POSITION OF THE DAY

POSITION OF THE DAY
PLAYBOOK
SEX EVERY DAY IN EVERY WAY

n FROM NERVE.COM

CHRONICLEBOOKS
SAN FRANCISCO

Library of Congress Cataloging-in-Publication Data available.
ISBN: 0-8118-4701-2

Manufactured in Canada

Designed by Erik Olsen Graphic Design

Distributed in Canada by Raincoast Books
9050 Shaughnessy Street
Vancouver, British Columbia V6P 6E5

10 9 8 7 6 5 4 3 2 1

Chronicle Books LLC
85 Second Street
San Francisco, California 94105

www.chroniclebooks.com

None of the people, products, or companies mentioned in this book in any way
endorse, support, promote, acknowledge, or have any connection whatsoever with
the content of the book, and no such endorsement or connection, express or implied,
is intended. Rather, the selection of names used in this book is the fanciful and
creative expression of its author.

INTRODUCTION

Welcome to *Position of the Day: Playbook*, Nerve.com's guide to a life of sexual inventiveness. When we published the first *Position of the Day*, we received a lot of feedback. Most of the people who bought the book were thrilled to have so many new ways to spice up their sex lives. Others said they loved the titles of the positions, but couldn't always manage to, *umm*, make them work right. A few people got stuck in the positions and were in need of emergency assistance.

We were especially surprised by how many questions people had about the positions: What are the pros and cons of doing "The Happy Fireman"? Do any of the positions work better with equipment — say a six-pack and a helmet? And, hey, do I still need to go to the gym if I'm regularly having sex upside down with my head on a chair and my feet wrapped around my lover's neck?

We've tried to address as many of these concerns as possible with our new edition, and the book now includes a handy rating system so you can keep track of which positions work best for you. Listing the equipment you might need and the various hazards and benefits of the different positions was easy. But questions about what sort of workout you get from having sex "every day in every way" kept us up at night worrying. After a hastily called meeting in the Nerve War Room, we decided to figure out how long the average sex act lasts and which muscles are used in a given position. We first compiled a mountain of data in the library and then sent a team of nimble and extremely attractive volunteers down to the laboratory. After strapping all sorts of wires to their bodies, and observing them having sex in hundreds of different positions, we remembered that we weren't scientists and just came up with our best estimates for the numbers of calories you'll burn.

We hope you'll have as much fun with this book as we had putting it together. And remember, if you happen to get stuck in any of the positions, a little melted butter can go a long way.

— The Nerve Staff

NERVE.COM

Nerve.com is the only intelligent magazine about sex and culture for women and men. Since 1997, Nerve has been publishing provocative essays, stimulating reporting, and sidesplitting commentary on a daily basis, as well as striking photographs of naked people that capture more than just their flesh. Described by *Entertainment Weekly* as "*Playboy*'s body with the *New Yorker*'s brain," Nerve has won numerous awards including a National Magazine Award nomination in 2000, Webby Awards in 2000 and 2001, and a *Forbes* "Best of the Web" selection in 2004. In recent years, Nerve has grown into a successful multimedia company, expanding into film, television, books, print, and online personals.

THE POSITIONS

JANUARY 01)
THE STROKE OF MIDNIGHT

CALORIES

Him 19

Her 13.6

EQUIPMENT

Champagne

Glasses

Confetti

BENEFIT

Fresh Start

○ Below Average

○ Average

○ Above Average

○ Whoa!

COMMENTS

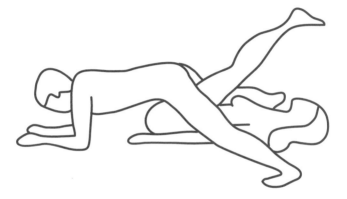

CALORIES

Him 75.6

Her 96

EQUIPMENT

Optional:

Newspaper

BENEFIT

Ideal for Less

Attractive Partners

○ Below Average

○ Average

○ Above Average

○ Whoa!

COMMENTS

JANUARY 03)
THE CHIMNEY SWEEP

CALORIES
Him 67.2
Her 48

EQUIPMENT
Chimney

HAZARD
Soot

○ Below Average
○ Average
○ Above Average
○ Whoa!

COMMENTS

THE MAGICIAN'S ASSISTANT

CALORIES
Him 100.8
Her 96

EQUIPMENT
Magic Wand

○ Below Average
○ Average
○ Above Average
○ Whoa!

COMMENTS

_____
_____
_____
_____
_____
_____

JANUARY 05)
THE SAN FRANCISCO TREAT

CALORIES

Him 19

Her 48

BENEFIT

Low Carb

○ Below Average

○ Average

○ Above Average

○ Whoa!

COMMENTS

_____

_____

_____

_____

_____

_____

CALORIES

Him 19

Her 54

○ Below Average

○ Average

○ Above Average

○ Whoa!

COMMENTS

JANUARY 07)
TICKLE ME, ELMO

CALORIES
Him 75.6
Her 54

HAZARD
Giggling Fits

○ Below Average
○ Average
○ Above Average
○ Whoa!

COMMENTS

_____
_____
_____
_____
_____
_____

JANUARY 08)
PUPPY LOVE

CALORIES

Giver   48

Receiver   48

○ Below Average

○ Average

○ Above Average

○ Whoa!

COMMENTS

JANUARY 09)
THE EDGE OF HIS SEAT

CALORIES

Him 117.6

Her 54

○ Below Average

○ Average

○ Above Average

○ Whoa!

COMMENTS

A MOVABLE FEAST

CALORIES
Him 67.2
Her 48

EQUIPMENT
Bed

○ Below Average
○ Average
○ Above Average
○ Whoa!

COMMENTS

JANUARY 11)
THE BOOT LICKER

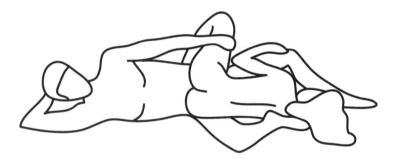

CALORIES

Him 19

Her 54

○ Below Average

○ Average

○ Above Average

○ Whoa!

COMMENTS

JANUARY 12)
"ARE THOSE COLORED CONTACTS?"

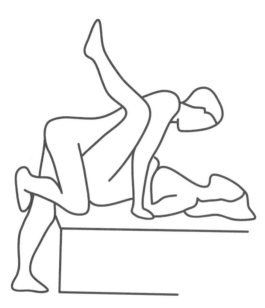

CALORIES	EQUIPMENT	
Him 75.6	Bed	○ Below Average
Her 54		○ Average
		○ Above Average
		○ Whoa!

COMMENTS

THE LONG GOODBYE

CALORIES

Him 75.6

Her 54

EQUIPMENT

Tissues

○ Below Average

○ Average

○ Above Average

○ Whoa!

COMMENTS

JANUARY 14)
THE FUNKY MONKEY

CALORIES	EQUIPMENT	
Him 75.6	Optional:	○ Below Average
Her 40	Banana	○ Average
		○ Above Average
		○ Whoa!

COMMENTS

JANUARY 15)
THE FOOT IN MOUTH

CALORIES

Giver   75.6

Receiver 67.2

○ Below Average

○ Average

○ Above Average

○ Whoa!

COMMENTS

_____

_____

_____

_____

_____

JANUARY 16)
THE FRAME JOB

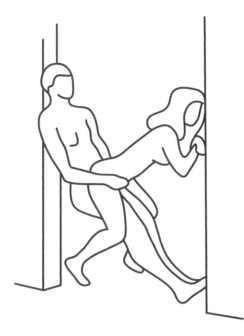

CALORIES
Him 66
Her 75.6

EQUIPMENT
Doorframe
Optional:
Leather Paddle
Nose Guard

HAZARD
Broken Nose

○ Below Average
○ Average
○ Above Average
○ Whoa!

COMMENTS

JANUARY 17)
STILL LIFE WITH PENETRATION

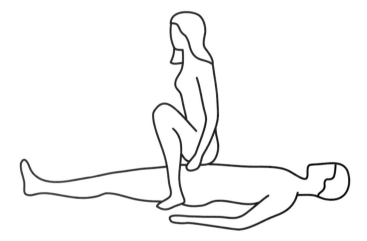

CALORIES

Him 19

Her 54

○ Below Average

○ Average

○ Above Average

○ Whoa!

COMMENTS

_____

_____

_____

_____

_____

JANUARY 18)
CAN YOU FEEL ME NOW?

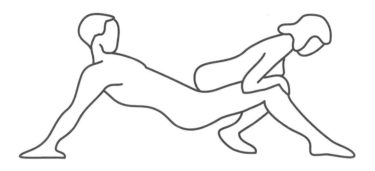

CALORIES
Him 75.6
Her 84

○ Below Average
○ Average
○ Above Average
○ Whoa!

COMMENTS

JANUARY 19)
BARTENDER, I'LL HAVE ANOTHER

CALORIES
Him 75.6
Her 54

EQUIPMENT
Barstool

○ Below Average
○ Average
○ Above Average
○ Whoa!

COMMENTS

THE OVER THE HILL

CALORIES

Him 75.6

Her 54

○ Below Average

○ Average

○ Above Average

○ Whoa!

COMMENTS

JANUARY 21)
THE PINK FLAMINGO

CALORIES

Him 19

Her 26

HAZARD

Leg Cramps

○ Below Average

○ Average

○ Above Average

○ Whoa!

COMMENTS

PULL ME UP, PULL ME DOWN

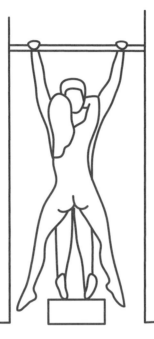

CALORIES
Him 134.4
Her 54

EQUIPMENT
Pull-up Bar
Stool
Deodorant

BENEFIT
Toned Biceps

○ Below Average
○ Average
○ Above Average
○ Whoa!

COMMENTS

JANUARY 23)
THE BARCALOUNGER

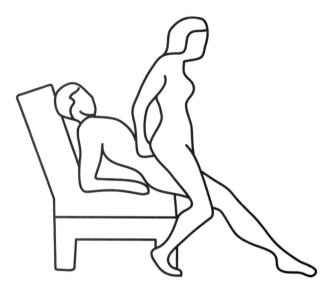

CALORIES

Him 75.6

Her 61

EQUIPMENT

Chair

O Below Average

O Average

O Above Average

O Whoa!

COMMENTS

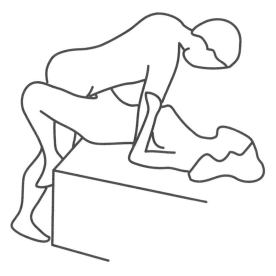

CALORIES

Him 75.6

Her 54

EQUIPMENT

Bed

Whipped Cream

○ Below Average

○ Average

○ Above Average

○ Whoa!

COMMENTS

JANUARY 25)
THE MAN FROM NANTUCKET

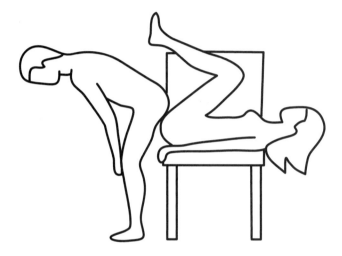

CALORIES

Him 75.6

Her 54

EQUIPMENT

Chair

○ Below Average

○ Average

○ Above Average

○ Whoa!

COMMENTS

JANUARY 26)
THE LOST IN TRANSLATION

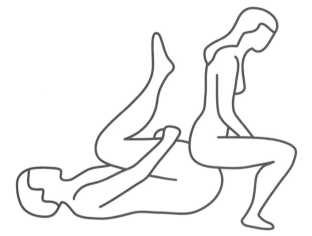

CALORIES

Him 19

Her 13.6

○ Below Average
○ Average
○ Above Average
○ Whoa!

COMMENTS

JANUARY 27)
THE UPSIDE-DOWN CAKE

CALORIES
Him 100.8
Her 72

EQUIPMENT
Wall

○ Below Average
○ Average
Ω Above Average
○ Whoa!

COMMENTS

IT'S FUN TO STAY AT THE Y...

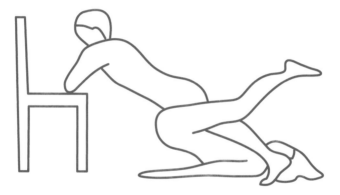

CALORIES	EQUIPMENT	
Him 134.4	Chair	○ Below Average
Her 96		○ Average
		○ Above Average
		○ Whoa!

COMMENTS

JANUARY 29)
MINDING THE GAP

CALORIES

Him 67.2

Her 72

EQUIPMENT

Counter

Bed

○ Below Average

○ Average

○ Above Average

○ Whoa!

COMMENTS

JANUARY 30)
THE MONKEY SEE MONKEY DO

CALORIES
Him 134.4
Her 54

EQUIPMENT
Pull-up Bar, Stool, Hand Powder
Optional: Gorilla Costume

○ Below Average
○ Average
○ Above Average
○ Whoa!

COMMENTS

JANUARY 31)
THE ASSIST

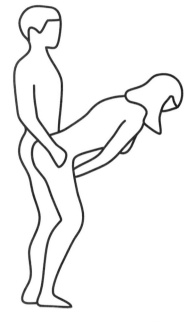

CALORIES

Him 75.6

Her   54

○ Below Average

○ Average

○ Above Average

○ Whoa!

COMMENTS

FEBRUARY 01)
THE HAND JIVE

CALORIES
Him 67.2
Her 54

EQUIPMENT
Bed

○ Below Average
○ Average
○ Above Average
○ Whoa!

COMMENTS

FEBRUARY 02)
THE BREAKFAST AT TIFFANY'S

CALORIES   **EQUIPMENT**

Him 54   Optional: Syrup

Her 19

○ Below Average

○ Average

○ Above Average

○ Whoa!

COMMENTS

FEBRUARY 03)
DOWN, BOY!

CALORIES	EQUIPMENT	
Him 94	Leash	○ Below Average
Her 65	Tranquilizer	○ Average
		○ Above Average
		○ Whoa!

COMMENTS

_____
_____
_____
_____
_____
_____

FEBRUARY 04)
THE KENTUCKY DERBY

CALORIES

Him 134.4

Her 96

EQUIPMENT

Optional:

Horsewhip

Riding Cap

HAZARD

Repeatedly Shouting
'Giddyap' May Turn
Off Some Women

○ Below Average
○ Average
○ Above Average
○ Whoa!

COMMENTS

DR. SCHOLL'S DAY OFF

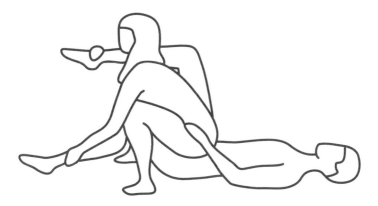

CALORIES

Him 62

Her 49

○ Below Average

○ Average

○ Above Average

○ Whoa!

COMMENTS

FEBRUARY 06)
THE FULLBACK

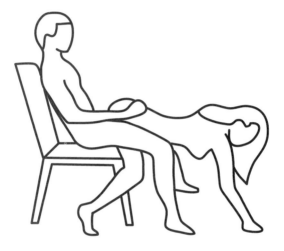

CALORIES **EQUIPMENT**
Him 19   Chair
Her 48

○ Below Average
○ Average
○ Above Average
○ Whoa!

COMMENTS

FEBRUARY 07)
THE EXECUTIVE PRIVILEGE

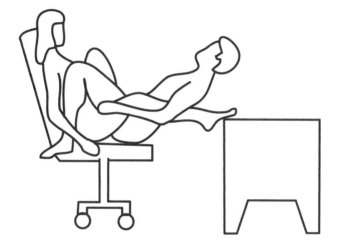

CALORIES
Him 67.2
Her 48

EQUIPMENT
Office Chair
Desk

○ Below Average
○ Average
○ Above Average
○ Whoa!

COMMENTS

FEBRUARY 08)
THE FORTUITOUS FAINT

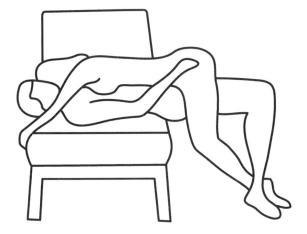

CALORIES

Him 19

Her 48

EQUIPMENT

Chair

○ Below Average

○ Average

○ Above Average

○ Whoa!

COMMENTS

FEBRUARY 09)
THE QUEEN OF THE HILL

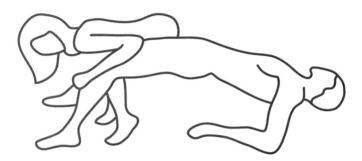

CALORIES

Him 66

Her 38

○ Below Average

○ Average

○ Above Average

○ Whoa!

COMMENTS

FEBRUARY 10)
THE "I THINK I'M STUCK"

CALORIES
Him 59
Her 46

EQUIPMENT
Chair

○ Below Average
○ Average
○ Above Average
○ Whoa!

COMMENTS

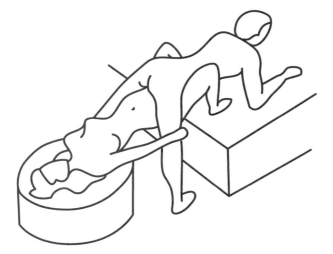

CALORIES

Him 75.6

Her 48

EQUIPMENT

Bed

Ottoman

○ Below Average

○ Average

○ Above Average

○ Whoa!

COMMENTS

FEBRUARY 12)
THE EDWARD SCISSORLEGS

CALORIES

Him 56

Her 78

EQUIPMENT

Bed

○ Below Average

○ Average

○ Above Average

○ Whoa!

COMMENTS

THE STRICTLY BALLROOM

CALORIES

Him 117.6

Her 96

EQUIPMENT

High Heels

Dance Music

○ Below Average

○ Average

○ Above Average

○ Whoa!

COMMENTS

FEBRUARY 14)
THE VERY HAPPY VALENTINE'S DAY

CALORIES

Him 83

Her 91

EQUIPMENT

Chair

Flowers

Chocolates

BENEFIT

True Love

○ Below Average

○ Average

○ Above Average

○ Whoa!

COMMENTS

FEBRUARY 15)
THE BLAZING SADDLES

CALORIES

Him 19

Her   48

O Below Average

O Average

O Above Average

O Whoa!

COMMENTS

FEBRUARY 16)
THE NOW WHAT?

CALORIES
Him 75.6
Her 48

EQUIPMENT
Rocking Chair

○ Below Average
○ Average
○ Above Average
○ Whoa!

COMMENTS

FEBRUARY 17)
THE UNBEARABLE
LIGHTNESS OF BEING

CALORIES

Him 100.8

Her 132

○ Below Average

○ Average

○ Above Average

○ Whoa!

COMMENTS

FEBRUARY 18)
BRINGING UP THE REAR

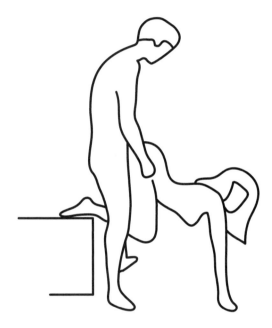

CALORIES   **EQUIPMENT**   ○ Below Average
Him 75.6   Bed   ○ Average
Her 54   ○ Above Average
                                ○ Whoa!

COMMENTS

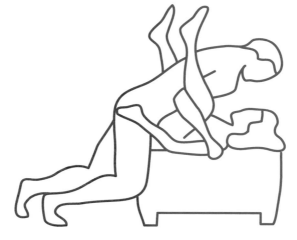

CALORIES
Him 75.6
Her 54

EQUIPMENT
Ottoman

○ Below Average
○ Average
○ Above Average
○ Whoa!

COMMENTS

ON TOP OF OLD SMOKEY

CALORIES

Him 67.2

Her 54

EQUIPMENT

Rocking Chair

○ Below Average

○ Average

○ Above Average

○ Whoa!

COMMENTS

THE BACKPEDALER

CALORIES
Him 67.2
Her 54

EQUIPMENT
Chair

○ Below Average
○ Average
○ Above Average
○ Whoa!

COMMENTS
_____
_____
_____
_____
_____
_____

FEBRUARY 22)
AMERICAN THIGH

FEBRUARY 23)
THE OVERZEALOUS
CONGRATULATIONS

CALORIES
Him 85
Her 43

EQUIPMENT
Stool

○ Below Average
○ Average
○ Above Average
○ Whoa!

COMMENTS

FEBRUARY 24)
THE MUSTANG SALLY

CALORIES

Him 168

Her 48

○ Below Average

○ Average

○ Above Average

○ Whoa!

COMMENTS

FEBRUARY 25)
THE ADULT SHOW AND TELL

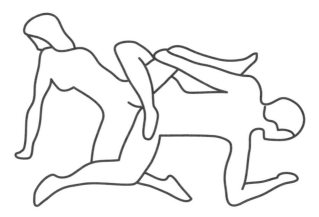

CALORIES

Him 70

Her 61

○ Below Average

○ Average

○ Above Average

○ Whoa!

COMMENTS

FEBRUARY 26)
ROCK ME, AMADEUS

CALORIES

Giver 50.4

Receiver 96

EQUIPMENT

Rocking Chair

Optional: Classical Music,
Powdered Wig, Baton

○ Below Average

○ Average

○ Above Average

○ Whoa!

COMMENTS

FEBRUARY 27)
BAD SANTA

CALORIES
Him 19
Her 54

EQUIPMENT
Rocking Chair

○ Below Average
○ Average
○ Above Average
○ Whoa!

COMMENTS

FEBRUARY 28)
THE NO ELBOWS ON
THE TABLE

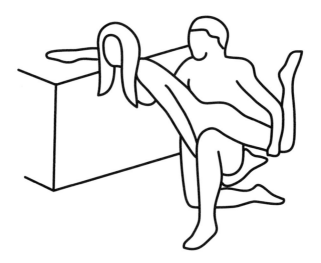

CALORIES
Him 75.6
Her 48

EQUIPMENT
Bed

○ Below Average
○ Average
○ Above Average
○ Whoa!

COMMENTS

MARCH 01)
THE CATCHER IN THE PIE

CALORIES

Him 66

Her 66

○ Below Average

○ Average

○ Above Average

○ Whoa!

COMMENTS

MARCH 02)
THE STAIRMASTER

CALORIES

Him 61

Her 70

EQUIPMENT

Stair

○ Below Average

○ Average

○ Above Average

○ Whoa!

COMMENTS

MARCH 03)
THE STARGAZER

CALORIES

Him 67.2

Her 96

HAZARD

Cloudy Nights

○ Below Average

○ Average

○ Above Average

○ Whoa!

COMMENTS

_____

_____

_____

_____

_____

_____

MARCH 04)
THE ARRIVALS TERMINAL

CALORIES   **HAZARD**

Him 75.6   Beeping Carts   ○ Below Average

Her 54   Security   ○ Average

                               ○ Above Average

                               ○ Whoa!

COMMENTS

MARCH 05)
THE SWING FLING

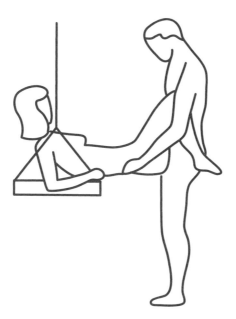

CALORIES
Him 75.6
Her   66

EQUIPMENT
Porch Swing

○ Below Average
○ Average
○ Above Average
○ Whoa!

COMMENTS

MARCH 06)
CROSSING THE LINE

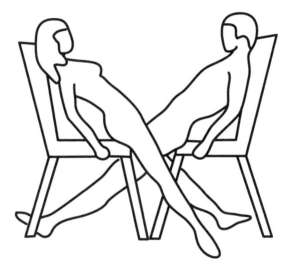

CALORIES   **EQUIPMENT**

Him 56   Two Chairs

Her 61

○ Below Average

○ Average

○ Above Average

○ Whoa!

COMMENTS

MARCH 07)
THE ROCK ME LIKE A
HURRICANE

CALORIES

Him 75.6

Her 96

EQUIPMENT

Rocking Chair

○ Below Average

○ Average

○ Above Average

○ Whoa!

COMMENTS

MARCH 08)
THE WHEELBARROW RACE

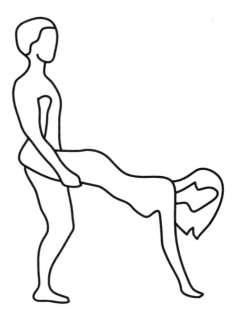

CALORIES

Him 100,8

Her 96

○ Below Average

○ Average

○ Above Average

○ Whoa!

COMMENTS

MARCH 09)
THE BUM DEAL

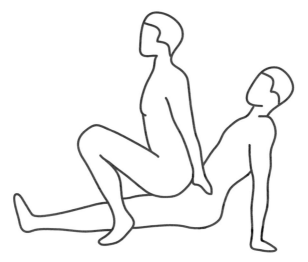

CALORIES

Giver   75.6

Receiver 75.6

○ Below Average

○ Average

○ Above Average

○ Whoa!

COMMENTS

MARCH 10)
PACKING THE SUITCASE

CALORIES

Him 117 ₆

Her 48

EQUIPMENT

Bed

○ Below Average

○ Average

◔ Above Average

○ Whoa!

COMMENTS

ASSEMBLY REQUIRED

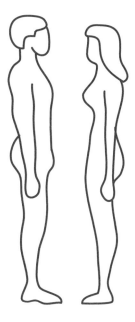

CALORIES

Him 19

Her 13.6

HAZARD

Intense Frustration

○ Below Average
○ Average
○ Above Average
○ Whoa!

COMMENTS

MARCH 12)
THE EXTENSION CORD

CALORIES

Him 117.6

Her 84

HAZARD

Electrocution

○ Below Average

○ Average

○ Above Average

○ Whoa!

COMMENTS

ADVENTURES IN BABYSITTING

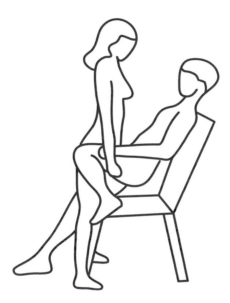

CALORIES	EQUIPMENT	
Him 55	Chair	○ Below Average
Her 60		○ Average
		○ Above Average
		○ Whoa!

COMMENTS

MARCH 14)
DINNER IS SERVED

CALORIES

Him 100.8

Her 96

EQUIPMENT

Butler's Uniform

○ Below Average

○ Average

○ Above Average

○ Whoa!

COMMENTS

THE WEEKEND AT BERNIE'S

CALORIES

Him 134.4

Her 72

EQUIPMENT

Sunglasses

○ Below Average

○ Average

○ Above Average

○ Whoa!

COMMENTS

MARCH 16)
THE FEEDING TROUGH

CALORIES

Him 75.6

Her 96

COMMENTS

○ Below Average

○ Average

○ Above Average

○ Whoa!

THE OUT OF TOWN GUESTS

CALORIES

Him (Give Only)	80
Him (Give and Take)	88.4
Her (Give and Take)	93
Her (Take Only)	54

BENEFIT

No Need for
Guest Bedroom

○ Below Average
○ Average
○ Above Average
○ Whoa!

COMMENTS

_____
_____
_____
_____
_____

MARCH 18)
THE SADIE HAWKINS

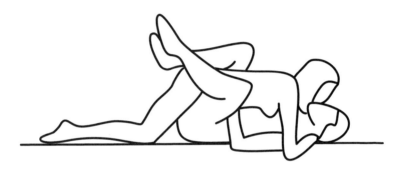

CALORIES

Him 75.6

Her 96

HAZARDS

Identity Crisis

Rug Burn

○ Below Average

○ Average

○ Above Average

○ Whoa!

COMMENTS

MARCH 19)
THE BUNNY SLOPE

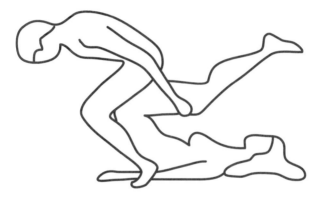

CALORIES   **EQUIPMENT**   ○ Below Average

Him 92.4   Ski Poles   ○ Average

Her   48   ○ Above Average

                                           ○ Whoa!

COMMENTS

_____

_____

_____

_____

_____

_____

MARCH 20)
THE DEMI AND ASHTON

CALORIES

Him 19

Her 54

○ Below Average

○ Average

◉ Above Average

○ Whoa!

COMMENTS

MARCH 21)
THE TWIST AND SHOUT

CALORIES   **EQUIPMENT**   **HAZARD**

Him 134.4   Advil   Getting Stuck

Her 96

○ Below Average
○ Average
○ Above Average
○ Whoa!

COMMENTS

_____
_____
_____
_____
_____
_____

MARCH 22)
THE PERPEN-DIC-ULAR

CALORIES

Him 75.6

Her 48

COMMENTS

○ Below Average

○ Average

◉ Above Average

○ Whoa!

THE "IT WASN'T ME"

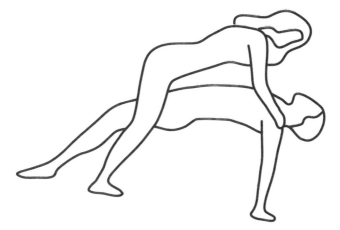

CALORIES	HAZARD	
Him 134.4	Him: Marks on the Neck	○ Below Average
Her 95	Premature Death	○ Average
	Her: Fingerprints	○ Above Average
		○ Whoa!

COMMENTS

_____
_____
_____
_____
_____
_____

MARCH 24)
THE FRIENDLY ASSASSIN

CALORIES

Him 19

Her 54

○ Below Average

○ Average

○ Above Average

○ Whoa!

COMMENTS

THE WHEN IN DOUBT

CALORIES	EQUIPMENT	HAZARD	
Him 75.6	Optional:	Boredom	○ Below Average
Her 54	Spiked Collar		○ Average
			○ Above Average
			○ Whoa!

COMMENTS

MARCH 26)
THE CROWDED SLEEPING CAR

CALORIES   **HAZARD**

Him 19   Falling Asleep

Her 13.6

○ Below Average

○ Average

○ Above Average

○ Whoa!

COMMENTS

THE NIP AND TUCK

CALORIES
Him 75.6
Her 66

EQUIPMENT
Pull-up Bar

○ Below Average
○ Average
○ Above Average
○ Whoa!

COMMENTS

MARCH 28)
THE PILATES CLASS

CALORIES
Him 75.6
Her 48

EQUIPMENT
Rocking Chair

○ Below Average
○ Average
○ Above Average
○ Whoa!

COMMENTS

MARCH 29)
THE VERY SPECIAL EPISODE

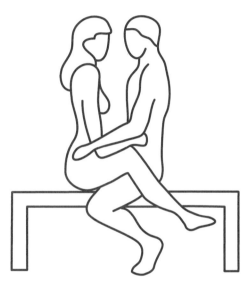

CALORIES	EQUIPMENT	
Him 19	Hanky	○ Below Average
Her 13.6	Table	○ Average
		○ Above Average
		○ Whoa!

COMMENTS

_____
_____
_____
_____
_____
_____

MARCH 30)
THE REVERSE WHEELBARROW

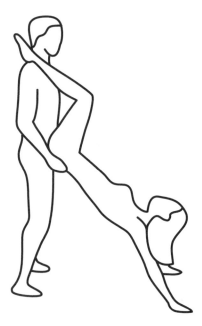

CALORIES

Him 100.8

Her 96

○ Below Average

○ Average

○ Above Average

○ Whoa!

COMMENTS

MARCH 31)
THE HOBBYHORSE

CALORIES
Him 117.6
Her 120

EQUIPMENT
Rocking Chair

○ Below Average
○ Average
○ Above Average
○ Whoa!

COMMENTS

APRIL 01)
APRIL FOOL'S PARADISE

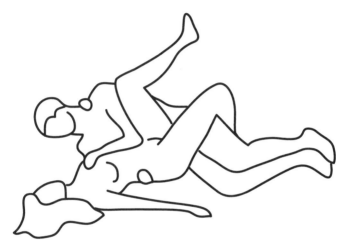

CALORIES

Him 75.6

Her 54

COMMENTS

○ Below Average

○ Average

◡ Above Average

○ Whoa!

THE WHEN HARRY MET SALLY

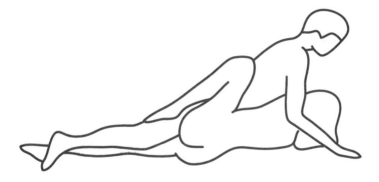

CALORIES

Him 75.6

Her   48

○ Below Average

○ Average

○ Above Average

○ Whoa!

COMMENTS

_____

_____

_____

_____

_____

_____

APRIL 03)
THE BLOCKING SLED

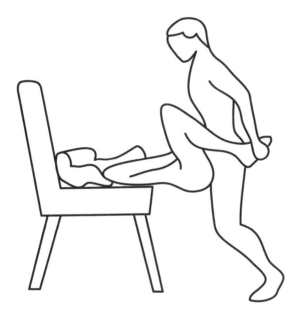

CALORIES
Him 75.6
Her 59

EQUIPMENT
Chair

○ Below Average
○ Average
↻ Above Average
○ Whoa!

COMMENTS

APRIL 04)
THE NIGHT CRAWLER

CALORIES   O Below Average

Him 67.2   O   Average

Her 48   O Above Average

                                O Whoa!

COMMENTS

_____
_____
_____
_____
_____
_____

APRIL 05)
MAN PROPOSES, WOMAN REACHES FOR MACE

CALORIES
Him 75.6
Her 48

EQUIPMENT
Bed

○ Below Average
○ Average
◉ Above Average
○ Whoa!

COMMENTS

APRIL 06)
THE FATAL ATTRACTION

CALORIES

Him 75.6

Her 13.6

EQUIPMENT

Oxygen Mask

O Below Average

O Average

O Above Average

O Whoa!

COMMENTS

APRIL 07)
THE SEARCH AND SEIZE-HER

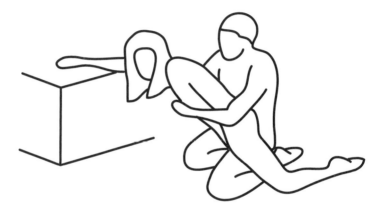

CALORIES

Him 75.6

Her 48

EQUIPMENT

Bed

○ Below Average

○ Average

○ Above Average

○ Whoa!

COMMENTS

THE LAMAZE COACH

CALORIES

Him 75.6

Her 54

HAZARD

Heavy Breathing

○ Below Average

○ Average

○ Above Average

○ Whoa!

COMMENTS

_____
_____
_____
_____
_____
_____

APRIL 09)
SOMETIMES YOU FEEL
LIKE A NUT

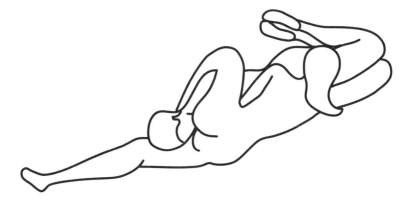

CALORIES

Him 67.2

Her 48

○ Below Average

○ Average

◐ Above Average

○ Whoa!

COMMENTS

_____
_____
_____
_____
_____

THE TOOTSIE ROLL

CALORIES

Him 75.6

Her 96

EQUIPMENT

Enormous Pipe

○ Below Average

○ Average

○ Above Average

○ Whoa!

COMMENTS

APRIL 11)
THE "I'LL BE BACK"

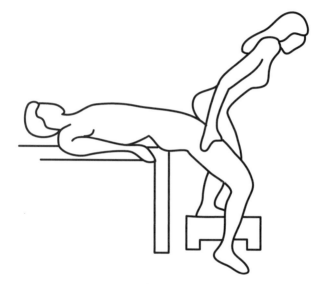

CALORIES

Him 19

Her 120

EQUIPMENT

Table

Stool

HAZARD

Schwarzenegger
Impersonations

○ Below Average

○ Average

○ Above Average

○ Whoa!

COMMENTS

APRIL 12)
THE RISING TIDE

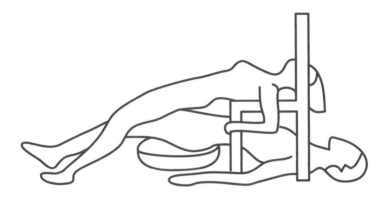

CALORIES	EQUIPMENT	
Him 19	Chair	○ Below Average
Her 48	Pillow	○ Average
		○ Above Average
		○ Whoa!

COMMENTS

APRIL 13)
THE REAR-ENDER

CALORIES

Him 75.6

Her 54

EQUIPMENT

Chair

O Below Average

O Average

O Above Average

O Whoa!

COMMENTS

APRIL 14)
SOUTHERN COMFORT

CALORIES

Him 75.6

Her 66

EQUIPMENT

Porch Swing

○ Below Average

○ Average

○ Above Average

○ Whoa!

COMMENTS

APRIL 15)
SIMON SAYS, "LAY DOWN WITH YOUR HEAD UNDER THE CHAIR"

CALORIES
Him 75.6
Her 54

EQUIPMENT
Chair

HAZARD
Listening to
Everything Simon
Says

○ Below Average
○ Average
◍ Above Average
○ Whoa!

COMMENTS

"ARE THOSE LEE PRESS-ONS?"

CALORIES

Him 67.2

Her 96

○ Below Average

○ Average

○ Above Average

○ Whoa!

COMMENTS

_____
_____
_____
_____
_____
_____

APRIL 17)
THE TWISTER STALEMATE

CALORIES   **EQUIPMENT**   ○ Below Average
Him 134.4   Twister Board   ○ Average
Her 96   Spinner   ○ Above Average
                                    ○ Whoa!

COMMENTS

THE TWIDDLING DEE

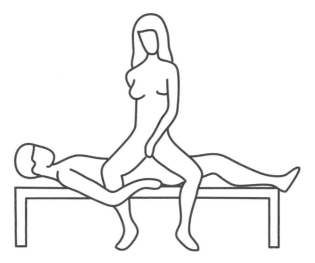

CALORIES

Him 19

Her 54

EQUIPMENT

Bench

○ Below Average

○ Average

○ Above Average

○ Whoa!

COMMENTS

APRIL 19)
THE SENATOR RICK SANTORUM

CALORIES   **EQUIPMENT**

Giver   100.8   Rocking Chair

Receiver   98

○ Below Average

○ Average

U Above Average

○ Whoa!

COMMENTS

CALORIES

Him 35

Her 22

○ Below Average

○ Average

○ Above Average

○ Whoa!

COMMENTS

APRIL 21)
THE HIND-QUARTERLY REVIEW

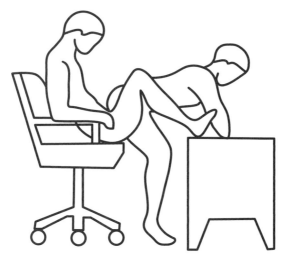

CALORIES

Giver   75.6

Receiver 54

EQUIPMENT

Chair

Desk

Door Lock

○ Below Average

○ Average

○ Above Average

○ Whoa!

COMMENTS

APRIL 22)
THE WALK HIM BACKWARDS
OVER THE PIPE TRICK

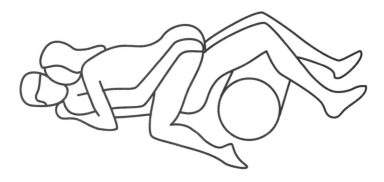

CALORIES

Him 67.2

Her 48

EQUIPMENT

Large Pipe

○ Below Average

○ Average

○ Above Average

○ Whoa!

COMMENTS

APRIL 23)
THE CHIROPRACTOR'S SECRET

CALORIES

Him 75.6

Her 54

EQUIPMENT

Chair

○ Below Average

○ Average

○ Above Average

○ Whoa!

COMMENTS

APRIL 24)
THE HAPPY CRASH TEST DUMMIES

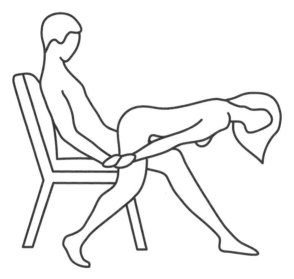

CALORIES
Him 75.6
Her 54

EQUIPMENT
Chair

○ Below Average
○ Average
○ Above Average
○ Whoa!

COMMENTS

APRIL 25)
CROUCHING TIGER, HIDDEN DRAGON

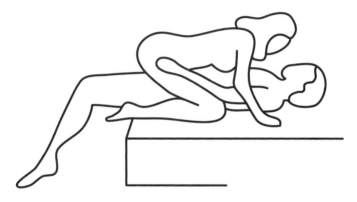

CALORIES

Him 19

Her 54

EQUIPMENT

Bed

Optional: Sword

○ Below Average

○ Average

○ Above Average

○ Whoa!

COMMENTS

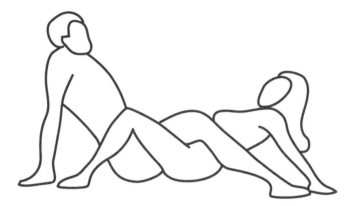

CALORIES

Him 67.2

Her   48

○ Below Average

○ Average

○ Above Average

○ Whoa!

COMMENTS

APRIL 27)
THE "YOU HAVE THE RIGHT TO REMAIN SILENT"

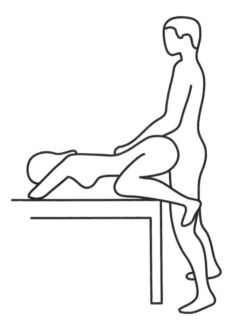

CALORIES
Him 75.6
Her 54

EQUIPMENT
Table
Optional: Police Uniform,
Baton, Handcuffs

○ Below Average
○ Average
○ Above Average
○ Whoa!

COMMENTS

APRIL 28)
THE ROCKER CHICK

CALORIES
Him 75.6
Her   48

EQUIPMENT
Rocking Chair

○ Below Average
○ Average
○ Above Average
○ Whoa!

COMMENTS

APRIL 29)
THE SLUNK HUNK

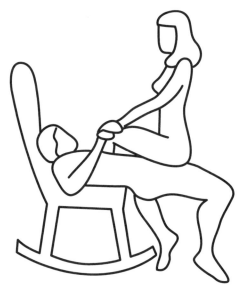

CALORIES

Him 19

Her 66

EQUIPMENT

Rocking Chair

○ Below Average
○ Average
○ Above Average
○ Whoa!

COMMENTS

APRIL 30)
BOBBING FOR CHERRIES

CALORIES

Giver　　54

Receiver　75.6

○ Below Average

○ Average

○ Above Average

○ Whoa!

COMMENTS

_____

_____

_____

_____

_____

_____

MAY 01)
THE BACKSLASH

CALORIES **EQUIPMENT**

Him 19 Table

Her 54

○ Below Average
○ Average
○ Above Average
○ Whoa!

COMMENTS

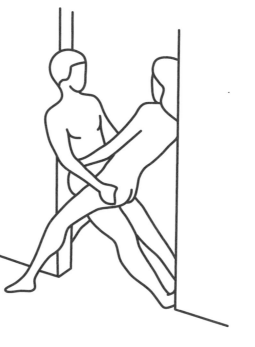

MAY 02)
THE HE WAS FRAMED

CALORIES
Him 55
Her 40

EQUIPMENT
Doorframe

○ Below Average
○ Average
○ Above Average
○ Whoa!

COMMENTS

MAY 03)
THE TAKES A LICKING

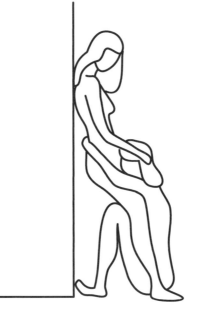

CALORIES

Giver 19

Receiver 13.6

EQUIPMENT

Wall

○ Below Average

○ Average

○ Above Average

○ Whoa!

COMMENTS

CALORIES
Him 75.6
Her 84

○ Below Average
○ Average
○ Above Average
○ Whoa!

COMMENTS

MAY 05)
THE HOME FITNESS TEST

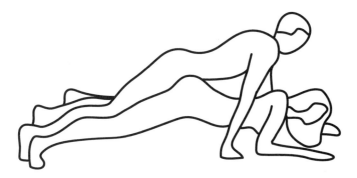

CALORIES

Him 134.4

Her 00

EQUIPMENT

Exercise Checklist

Whistle

○ Below Average

○ Average

◐ Above Average

○ Whoa!

COMMENTS

WHAT WOULD YOU DO FOR A KLONDIKE BAR?

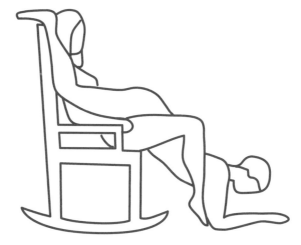

CALORIES
Him 75.6
Her 48

EQUIPMENT
Rocking Chair

BENEFIT
Klondike Bar

○ Below Average
○ Average
○ Above Average
○ Whoa!

COMMENTS

MAY 07)
THE BENDS

CALORIES

Giver   13.6

Receiver 54

COMMENTS

○ Below Average
○ Average
○ Above Average
○ Whoa!

THE NOT SO FAST, MISSY

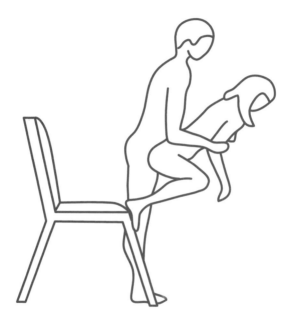

CALORIES
Him 100.8
Her 120

EQUIPMENT
Chair

○ Below Average
○ Average
○ Above Average
○ Whoa!

COMMENTS

MAY 09)
THE MUSICAL CHAIRS
CONSOLATION PRIZE

CALORIES

Him 50

Her 72

EQUIPMENT

Chair

○ Below Average

○ Average

○ Above Average

○ Whoa!

COMMENTS

MAY 10)
THE WHILE YOU WERE SLEEPING

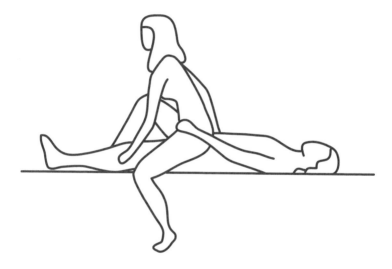

CALORIES
Him 19
Her 48

EQUIPMENT
Optional:
Sleeping Pills

BENEFIT
No Performance Anxiety

○ Below Average
○ Average
○ Above Average
○ Whoa!

COMMENTS

MAY 11)
SPLENDOR IN THE ASS

CALORIES

Him 73

Her 90

EQUIPMENT

Rocking Chair

○ Below Average
○ Average
○ Above Average
○ Whoa!

COMMENTS

THE GOOD CONVERSATIONALIST

CALORIES
Him 67.2
Her 48

EQUIPMENT
Thesaurus

BENEFIT
Improved Vocabulary

○ Below Average
○ Average
○ Above Average
○ Whoa!

COMMENTS

_____
_____
_____
_____
_____
_____

MAY 13)
SHOULDERING THE BURDEN

CALORIES

Him 75.6

Her 54

○ Below Average

○ Average

○ Above Average

○ Whoa!

COMMENTS

MAY 14)
THE GOOD TO THE LAST
DROP FEELING

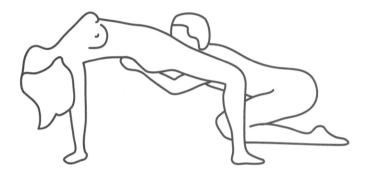

CALORIES

Him 72

Her 88

○ Below Average

○ Average

○ Above Average

○ Whoa!

COMMENTS

_____

_____

_____

_____

_____

_____

MAY 15)
THE "HI THERE"

CALORIES

Him 54

Her 38

EQUIPMENT

Rocking Chair

○ Below Average

○ Average

○ Above Average

○ Whoa!

COMMENTS

CALORIES

Giver   50.4

Receiver 75.6

O Below Average

O Average

O Above Average

O Whoa!

COMMENTS

MAY 17)
SHE'S THE KING OF THE WORLD

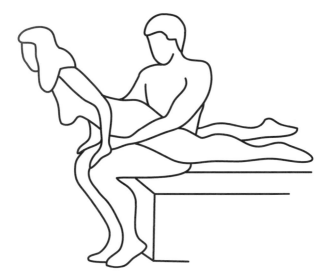

CALORIES
Him 19
Her 48

EQUIPMENT
Bed

○ Below Average
○ Average
○ Above Average
○ Whoa!

COMMENTS

MAY 18)
THE RIDE OF HIS LIFE

CALORIES   **EQUIPMENT**   **HAZARD**   ○ Below Average

Him 49   Rocking Chair   Strained Calves   ○ Average

Her 54   ○ Above Average

                                                                  ○ Whoa!

COMMENTS

MAY 19)
THE ONLY CHAIR IN THE HOUSE TRICK

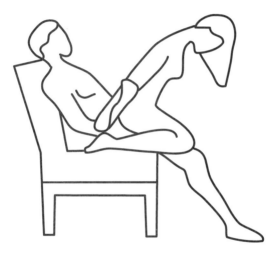

CALORIES
Him 67.2
Her 96

EQUIPMENT
Chair

O Below Average
O Average
O Above Average
O Whoa!

COMMENTS

MAY 20)
THE FOR WHOM THE
BELL TOLLS

CALORIES	EQUIPMENT	
Him 50.4	Rope, Doorframe,	○ Below Average
Her 48	Earplugs, Bell	○ Average
		○ Above Average
		○ Whoa!

COMMENTS

MAY 21)
THE HEAD SHOULDERS
KNEES AND TOES

CALORIES

Him 75.6

Her 54

○ Below Average

○ Average

○ Above Average

○ Whoa!

COMMENTS

_____
_____
_____
_____
_____

CALORIES
Him 57
Her 51

EQUIPMENT
Rocking Chair

BENEFIT
Guaranteed to
Get a 'Whoa'

O Below Average
O Average
O Above Average
O Whoa!

COMMENTS

MAY 23)
THE OLD "LET'S JUST CUDDLE" LINE

CALORIES

Him 67.2

Her 48

O Below Average

O Average

O Above Average

O Whoa!

COMMENTS

THE SPECIAL K

CALORIES

Giver   75.6

Receiver 54

EQUIPMENT

Stool

O Below Average

O Average

O Above Average

O Whoa!

COMMENTS

MAY 25)
SEX ON THE BRAIN

CALORIES

Him 75.4

Her 82

HAZARD

Stiff Neck

○ Below Average

○ Average

○ Above Average

○ Whoa!

COMMENTS

THE MRS. ROBINSON

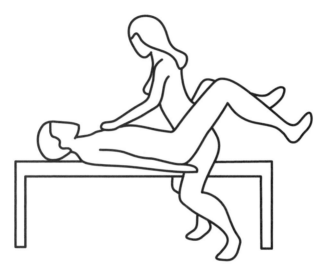

CALORIES

Him 67.2

Her 66

EQUIPMENT

Bench

○ Below Average

○ Average

○ Above Average

○ Whoa!

COMMENTS

MAY 27)
THE LORD OF THE RINGS

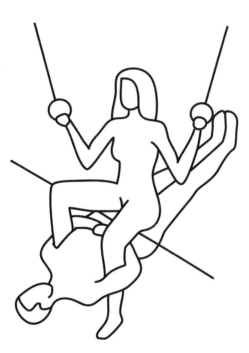

CALORIES   **EQUIPMENT**   **HAZARD**

Him 167.2   Gym   Gym Membership   O Below Average
Her 132   Rings   Revoked   O Average
                                                   O Above Average
                                                   O Whoa!

COMMENTS

MAY 28)
THE MEATBALL

CALORIES   **HAZARD**   O Below Average
Him 50.4   Rolling Off the Bed   O Average
Her 48   O Above Average
                                             O Whoa!

COMMENTS

MAY 29)
THE "MY WHAT BIG EYES YOU HAVE"

CALORIES

Him 67.2

Her 84

O Below Average

O Average

O Above Average

O Whoa!

COMMENTS

CALORIES

Him 19

Her 54

EQUIPMENT

Tuffet

O Below Average

O Average

O Above Average

O Whoa!

COMMENTS

MAY 31)
THE NEW APPRENTICE

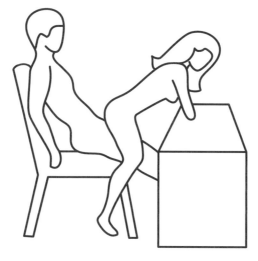

CALORIES	EQUIPMENT	BENEFIT	
Him 75.6	Chair	Job as President	○ Below Average
Her 54	Desk	of a Trump Company	○ Average
			○ Above Average
			○ Whoa!

COMMENTS

JUNE 01)
YOU DO THE HOKEY POKEY AND YOU...

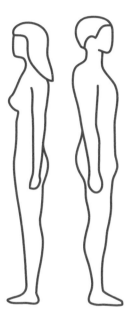

CALORIES
Him 19
Her 13.6

HAZARD
Confusion
Loneliness

○ Below Average
○ Average
○ Above Average
○ Whoa!

COMMENTS

JUNE 02)
HOW DR. HEIMLICH GOT HIS BIG IDEA

CALORIES
Him 19
Her 48

EQUIPMENT
Mattress

HAZARD
Vomiting

O Below Average
O Average
O Above Average
O Whoa!

COMMENTS

JUNE 03)
THE WINDOW WASHER

CALORIES	EQUIPMENT	
Him 67.2	Stool	O Below Average
Her 96	Wall	O Average
		O Above Average
		O Whoa!

COMMENTS

JUNE 04)
THE DOG AND PONY SHOW

CALORIES

Him 92.4

Her 84

○ Below Average

○ Average

○ Above Average

○ Whoa!

COMMENTS

JUNE 05)
THE HUMPTY DUMPTY

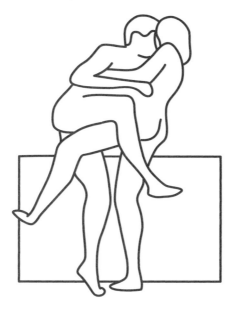

CALORIES

Him 67.8

Her 48

EQUIPMENT

Wall

HAZARD

Falling Off the Wall

O Below Average

O Average

O Above Average

O Whoa!

COMMENTS

JUNE 06)
THE CLEANING SERVICE

CALORIES
Him 100.8
Her 96

BENEFIT
Two Birds with One Stone

○ Below Average
○ Average
○ Above Average
○ Whoa!

COMMENTS

JUNE 07)
THE IRONING BOARD

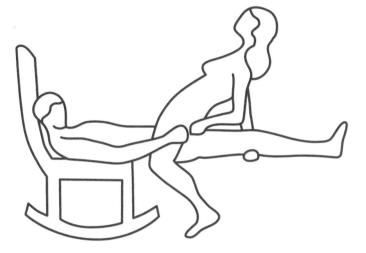

CALORIES
Him 67.2
Her 96

EQUIPMENT
Rocking Chair

O Below Average
O Average
O Above Average
O Whoa!

COMMENTS

JUNE 08)
THE HANG BANG

CALORIES
Him 112
Her   96

EQUIPMENT
Chair
Pull-up Bar

O Below Average
O Average
O Above Average
O Whoa!

COMMENTS

THE PINBALL WIZARD

CALORIES
Him 67.2
Her 48

EQUIPMENT
Bed

HAZARD
Do Not Tilt

O Below Average
O Average
O Above Average
O Whoa!

COMMENTS

JUNE 10)
THE GOOD FENG SHUI

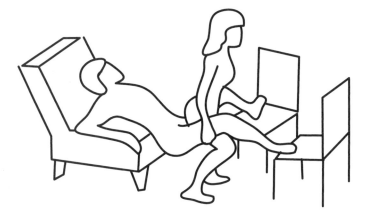

CALORIES
Him 67.2
Her 66

EQUIPMENT
Three Chairs

BENEFIT
No Need to
Rearrange Furniture

○ Below Average
○ Average
○ Above Average
○ Whoa!

COMMENTS

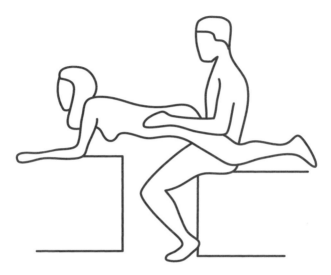

CALORIES
Him 19
Her 48

EQUIPMENT
Two Beds

O Below Average
O Average
O Above Average
O Whoa!

COMMENTS

JUNE 12)
OBEY YOUR THIRST

CALORIES

Him 19

Her   48

○ Below Average
○ Average
○ Above Average
○ Whoa!

COMMENTS

JUNE 13)
THE BONGO PLAYER

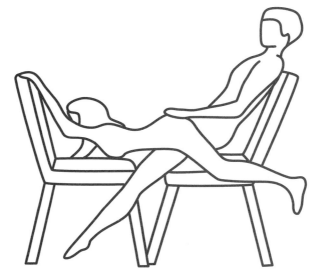

CALORIES	EQUIPMENT	BENEFIT	
Him 19	Two Chairs	Saves Time on	○ Below Average
Her 54		Drumming Practice	○ Average
			○ Above Average
			○ Whoa!

COMMENTS

JUNE 14)
YOU MAY APPROACH
THE BENCH

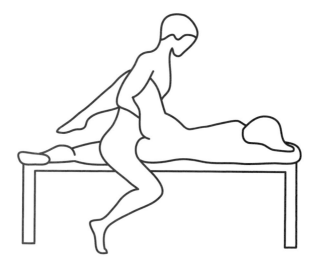

CALORIES   **EQUIPMENT**

Him 75.6   Bench

Her 48

○ Below Average

○ Average

○ Above Average

○ Whoa!

COMMENTS

JUNE 15)
THE RIGHT ANGLE STUFF

CALORIES
Him 67.2
Her 66

EQUIPMENT
Two Beds

O Below Average
O Average
O Above Average
O Whoa!

COMMENTS

JUNE 16)
THE STANDING ROOM ONLY

CALORIES

Him 75.6

Her 66

EQUIPMENT

Wall

○ Below Average
○ Average
○ Above Average
○ Whoa!

COMMENTS

JUNE 17)
THE HORNY TOAD

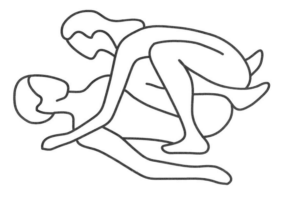

CALORIES

Him 55

Her 72

O Below Average

O Average

O Above Average

O Whoa!

COMMENTS

JUNE 18)
IF YOU'RE HAPPY AND YOU KNOW IT HOLD YOUR LEG

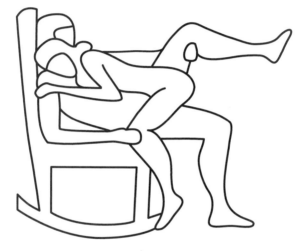

CALORIES

Him 75.6

Her 54

EQUIPMENT

Rocking Chair

O Below Average

O Average

O Above Average

O Whoa!

COMMENTS

JUNE 19)
THE ROCKETTE CHOREOGRAPHER

CALORIES
Him 67.2
Her 48

EQUIPMENT
Tights
High Heels
Show Tunes

O Below Average
O Average
O Above Average
O Whoa!

COMMENTS

JUNE 20)
THE FROM HERE TO ETERNITY

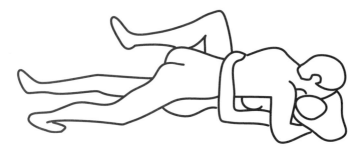

CALORIES
Him 75.6
Her 66

EQUIPMENT
Cheesy Music

O Below Average
O Average
O Above Average
O Whoa!

COMMENTS

JUNE 21)
THE BACKSEAT DRIVE-HER

CALORIES	EQUIPMENT	
Him 19	Chair	O Below Average
Her 54		O Average
		O Above Average
		O Whoa!

COMMENTS

JUNE 22)
THE ANGRY WHITE MALE

CALORIES

Him 75.6

Her 54

EQUIPMENT

Bed

○ Below Average

○ Average

○ Above Average

○ Whoa!

COMMENTS

JUNE 23)
THE OEDIPUS COMPLEX

CALORIES

Him 19

Her 72

EQUIPMENT

Wall

Optional:

Pacifier

HAZARD

Dirty Diapers

○ Below Average

○ Average

○ Above Average

○ Whoa!

COMMENTS

JUNE 24)
THE ESCAPE IS FUTILE

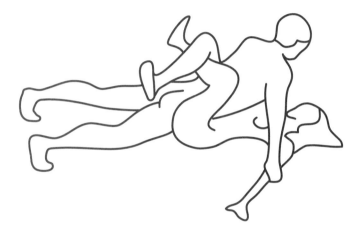

CALORIES

Him 75.6

Her 54

O Below Average

O Average

O Above Average

O Whoa!

COMMENTS

JUNE 25)
THE KNEE-JERK REACTION

CALORIES
Him 75.6
Her 54

EQUIPMENT
Bench

O Below Average
O Average
O Above Average
O Whoa!

COMMENTS

JUNE 26)
THE FIREMAN'S POLE

CALORIES   **EQUIPMENT**

Him 75.6   Pole

Her 54

O Below Average

O Average

O Above Average

O Whoa!

COMMENTS

JUNE 27)
THE "HONEY, I'M HOME"

CALORIES

Him 100.8

Her   66

○ Below Average

○ Average

○ Above Average

○ Whoa!

COMMENTS

JUNE 28)
THE BREAK A LEG

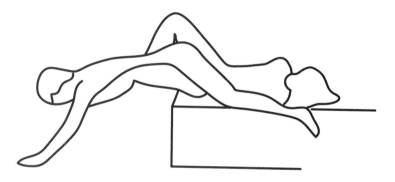

CALORIES   **EQUIPMENT**   ○ Below Average
Him 75.4   Mattress   ○ Average
Her 54   ○ Above Average
                                                             ○ Whoa!

COMMENTS

JUNE 29)
THE LOCK 'N' LOAD

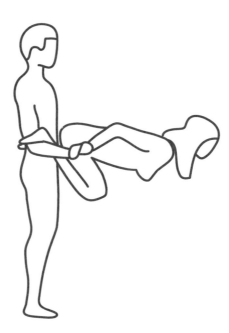

CALORIES

Him 100.8

Her   132

○ Below Average

○ Average

○ Above Average

○ Whoa!

COMMENTS

JUNE 30)
THE FACIAL

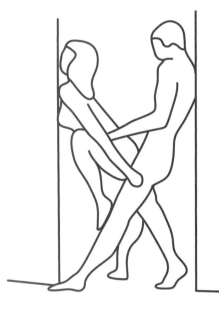

CALORIES
Him 75.6
Her 66

EQUIPMENT
Doorframe

○ Below Average
○ Average
○ Above Average
○ Whoa!

COMMENTS

CALORIES
Him 19
Her   60

EQUIPMENT
Rocking Chair

O Below Average
O Average
O Above Average
O Whoa!

COMMENTS

JULY 02)
CREW PRACTICE

CALORIES
Him 67.2
Her 54

EQUIPMENT
Chair

O Below Average
O Average
O Above Average
O Whoa!

COMMENTS

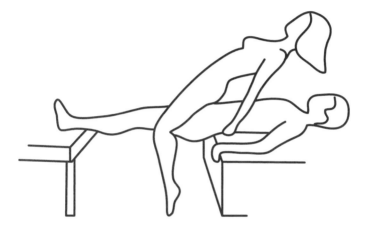

CALORIES

Him 67.2

Her 96

EQUIPMENT

Bed

Desk

○ Below Average

○ Average

○ Above Average

○ Whoa!

COMMENTS

JULY 04)
THE FOURTH OF JULY HOTDOG

CALORIES

Him 75.6

Her 66

O Below Average

O Average

O Above Average

O Whoa!

COMMENTS

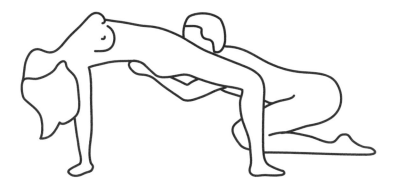

CALORIES

Him 72

Her 88

○ Below Average

○ Average

○ Above Average

○ Whoa!

COMMENTS

JULY 06)
THE LUMBERJACK AND JILL

CALORIES

Him 117.6

Her 84

EQUIPMENT

Rocking Chair

○ Below Average

○ Average

○ Above Average

○ Whoa!

COMMENTS

JULY 07)
THE CRUNCH AND MUNCH

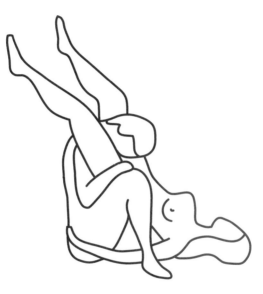

CALORIES

Him 67.2

Her 96

○ Below Average

○ Average

○ Above Average

○ Whoa!

COMMENTS

JULY 08)
THE U-TURN

CALORIES
Him 75.4
Her   66

EQUIPMENT
Rocking Chair

O Below Average
O Average
O Above Average
O Whoa!

COMMENTS

JULY 09)
THE MUD FLAPPER

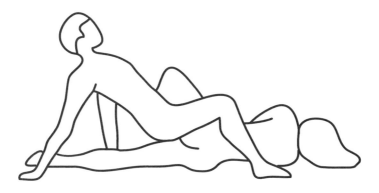

CALORIES

Him 75.6

Her   51

○ Below Average

○ Average

○ Above Average

○ Whoa!

COMMENTS

JULY 10)
THE PRESSED SHIRT

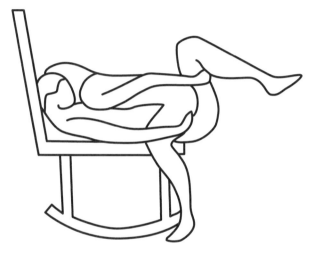

CALORIES
Him 67.2
Her 54

EQUIPMENT
Steaming,
Hot Bodies

BENEFIT
No Need for
Ironing

○ Below Average
○ Average
○ Above Average
○ Whoa!

COMMENTS

JULY 11)
THE BARYSHNIKOV

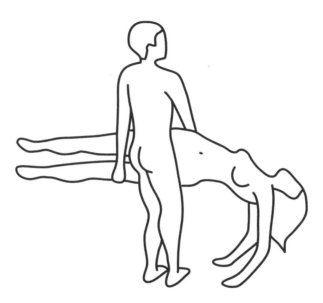

CALORIES

Him 100.6

Her 96

EQUIPMENT

Optional:

Leotard

O Below Average

O Average

O Above Average

O Whoa!

COMMENTS

_____
_____
_____
_____
_____
_____

THE GIRLS JUST WANT TO HAVE FUN

CALORIES

Her 61

Her 61

EQUIPMENT

Two Chairs

○ Below Average

○ Average

○ Above Average

○ Whoa!

COMMENTS

THE LONELY WIFE

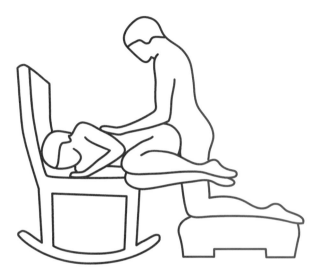

CALORIES	EQUIPMENT	
Him 75.6	Chair	○ Below Average
Her 48	Stool	○ Average
		○ Above Average
		○ Whoa!

COMMENTS

JULY 14)
THE "DUDE, WHERE'S YOUR HAND?"

CALORIES
Him 50.4
Her 54

EQUIPMENT
Rocking Chair

HAZARD
Getting Stuck

O Below Average
O Average
O Above Average
O Whoa!

COMMENTS

JULY 15)
THE WET DREAMER

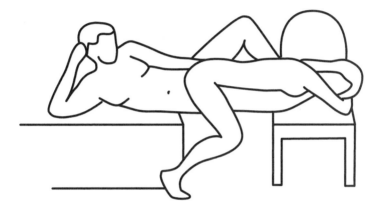

CALORIES	EQUIPMENT	
Him 19	Chair	O Below Average
Her 66	Bed	O Average
		O Above Average
		O Whoa!

COMMENTS

JULY 16)
THE EM-IN-EM

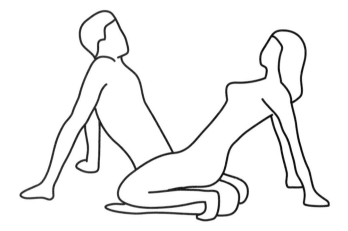

CALORIES

Him 67.2

Her 48

○ Below Average

○ Average

○ Above Average

○ Whoa!

COMMENTS

CALORIES

Him 19

Her 36

○ Below Average

○ Average

○ Above Average

○ Whoa!

COMMENTS

JULY 18)
THE OLD AND THE RESTLESS

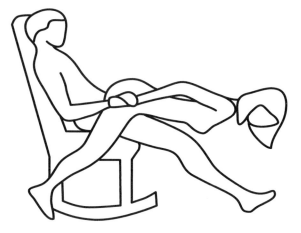

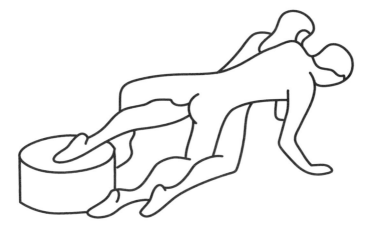

CALORIES **EQUIPMENT**   O Below Average
Him 92.9   Stool   O Average
Her 66   O Above Average
                O Whoa!

COMMENTS

JULY 20)
THE SIDESWIPE

CALORIES

Him 54

Her 63

○ Below Average

○ Average

○ Above Average

○ Whoa!

COMMENTS

JULY 21)
WAITING TO EXHALE

CALORIES	HAZARD	
Him 19	Him: Suffocation	O Below Average
Her 54	Her: Involuntary Manslaughter	O Average
		O Above Average
		O Whoa!

COMMENTS

JULY 22)
NAP TIME

CALORIES

Him 19

Her 13.6

EQUIPMENT

Pillow

○ Below Average

○ Average

○ Above Average

○ Whoa!

COMMENTS

THE STEAM CLEANER

CALORIES   **EQUIPMENT**   ○ Below Average
Him 75.6   Rocking Chair   ○ Average
Her 54   ○ Above Average
                                        ○ Whoa!

COMMENTS

JULY 24)
THE "HOLD IT RIGHT THERE"

CALORIES

Him 75.6

Her   48

○ Below Average

○ Average

○ Above Average

○ Whoa!

COMMENTS

THE DOCTOR STRANGE LOVE

CALORIES	EQUIPMENT	
Him 75.6	Chair	O Below Average
Her 54		O Average
		O Above Average
		O Whoa!

COMMENTS

JULY 26)
THE "DO'H"

CALORIES	EQUIPMENT	HAZARD	
Him 75.6	Wall	Concussion	○ Below Average
Her 54		Chipped Paint	○ Average
			○ Above Average
			○ Whoa!

COMMENTS

CALORIES

Him 134.4

Her 72

○ Below Average

○ Average

○ Above Average

○ Whoa!

COMMENTS

JULY 28)
THE BACKPACKER

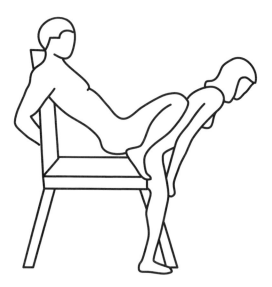

CALORIES **EQUIPMENT**

Him 119.6   Chair

Her 48

○ Below Average

○ Average

○ Above Average

○ Whoa!

COMMENTS

JULY 29)
THE "YOU MAY KISS THE BRIDE"

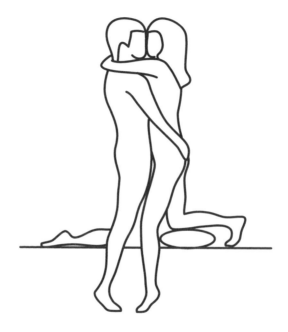

CALORIES

Him 19.19

Her 13.6

EQUIPMENT

Pillow

○ Below Average

○ Average

○ Above Average

○ Whoa!

COMMENTS

JULY 30)
THE "GENTLEMEN, START YOUR ENGINES"

CALORIES

Giver 75.6

Giver and Receiver 94

Receiver 52

EQUIPMENT

Coffee Table

○ Below Average

○ Average

○ Above Average

○ Whoa!

COMMENTS

THE CLOTHESLINE PIN

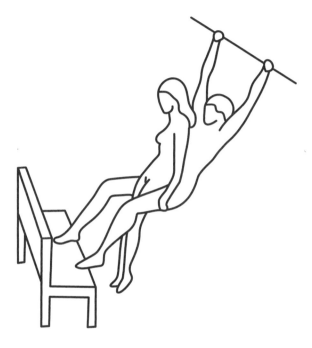

CALORIES	EQUIPMENT	
Him 134.4	Clothesline	○ Below Average
Her 54	Bench	○ Average
		○ Above Average
		○ Whoa!

COMMENTS

AUGUST 01)
THE DRAGONFLY

CALORIES

Him 75.6

Her 96

○ Below Average
○ Average
○ Above Average
○ Whoa!

COMMENTS

LAP OF LUXURY

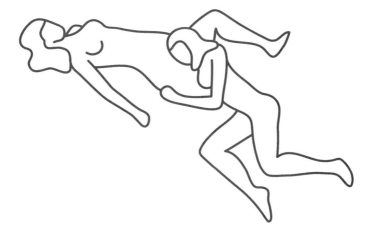

CALORIES

Giver   48

Receiver   48

○ Below Average

○ Average

○ Above Average

○ Whoa!

COMMENTS

AUGUST 03)
THE "IT'S A BOY"

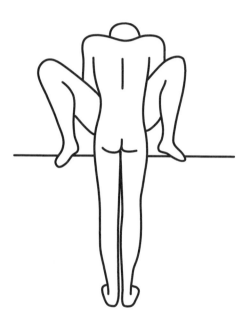

CALORIES
Him 75.6
Her 54

EQUIPMENT
Table

O Below Average
O Average
O Above Average
O Whoa!

COMMENTS

AUGUST 04)
THE MULTITASKING
PEDICURIST

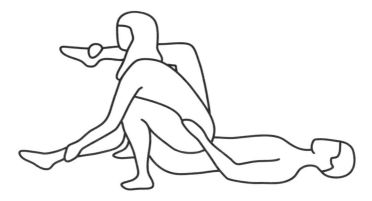

CALORIES
Him 62
Her   49

O Below Average
O Average
O Above Average
O Whoa!

COMMENTS

AUGUST 05)
THE CROWDED SUBWAY

CALORIES

Him 50.4

Her 54

O Below Average

O Average

O Above Average

O Whoa!

COMMENTS

CALORIES
Him 92.4
Her 96

EQUIPMENT
Bed

○ Below Average
○ Average
○ Above Average
○ Whoa!

COMMENTS

AUGUST 07)
KNOCKING ON HEAVEN'S DOOR

CALORIES

Him 75.6

Her 66

EQUIPMENT

Doorframe

O Below Average

O Average

O Above Average

O Whoa!

COMMENTS

THE BEST PART OF WAKING UP

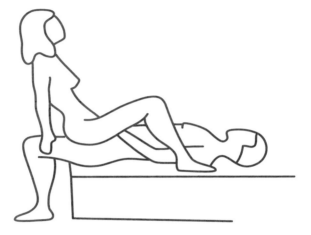

CALORIES

Him 67.2

Her 54

EQUIPMENT

Bed

O Below Average

O Average

O Above Average

O Whoa!

COMMENTS

AUGUST 09)
THE I WANNA ROCK WITH YOU

CALORIES

Him 75.6

Her 54

EQUIPMENT

Rocking Chair

○ Below Average

○ Average

○ Above Average

○ Whoa!

COMMENTS

AUGUST 10)
THE MASSEUSE GOOSE

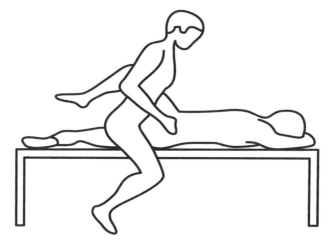

CALORIES
Giver   75.6
Receiver 19

EQUIPMENT
Massage Table

BENEFIT
Loose Muscles

O Below Average
O Average
O Above Average
O Whoa!

COMMENTS

AUGUST 11)
THE RUNNING WITH SCISSORS

CALORIES

Him 75.6

Her 96

○ Below Average

○ Average

○ Above Average

○ Whoa!

COMMENTS

THE BENCH PRESS

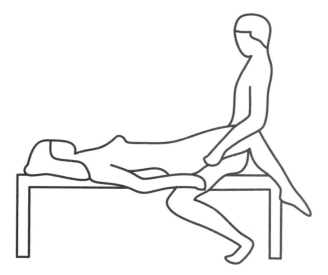

CALORIES
Him 88
Her 54

EQUIPMENT
Bench

○ Below Average
○ Average
○ Above Average
○ Whoa!

COMMENTS

AUGUST 13)
THE DEPRESSED DOGGIE

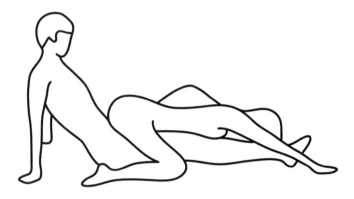

CALORIES

Him 75.6

Her 48

○ Below Average

○ Average

○ Above Average

○ Whoa!

COMMENTS

AUGUST 14)
THE DRAG QUEEN

CALORIES

Him 134.4

Her 72

O Below Average

O Average

O Above Average

O Whoa!

COMMENTS

AUGUST 15)
THE TO EACH HIS OWN

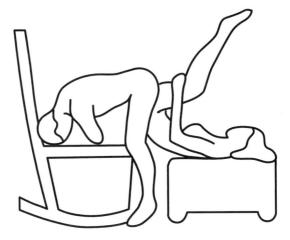

CALORIES

Him 67.2

Her 48

EQUIPMENT

Rocking Chair

Ottoman

HAZARD

Explaining Position
to Partner

○ Below Average

○ Average

○ Above Average

○ Whoa!

COMMENTS

AUGUST 16)
THE INDECENT PROPOSAL

CALORIES	EQUIPMENT	HAZARD	
Him 67.2	Ring	Monogamy	O Below Average
Her 48	Optional:		O Average
	Prenuptial Agreement		O Above Average
			O Whoa!

COMMENTS

AUGUST 17)
THE THIS LITTLE PIGGY

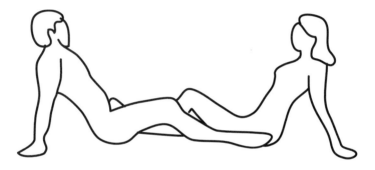

CALORIES

Him 19

Her 13.6

EQUIPMENT

Optional:

Nail Clipper

Pumice Stone

HAZARD

Long Toenails

○ Below Average

○ Average

○ Above Average

○ Whoa!

COMMENTS

AUGUST 18)
THE WE'RE NOT WORTHY

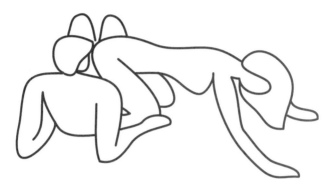

CALORIES

Him 92.4

Her 66

○ Below Average

○ Average

○ Above Average

○ Whoa!

COMMENTS

AUGUST 19)
THE DOCTOR IS IN

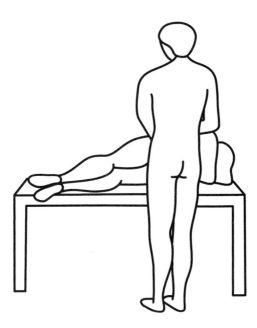

CALORIES

Him 75.6

Her 54

EQUIPMENT

Table

Optional: White Doctor's Coat,
Stethoscope

○ Below Average

○ Average

○ Above Average

○ Whoa!

COMMENTS

AUGUST 20)
THE INSIDE VIEW

CALORIES
Him 85
Her 54

EQUIPMENT
Rocking Chair

○ Below Average
○ Average
○ Above Average
○ Whoa!

COMMENTS

AUGUST 21)
THE BACK CRACKER

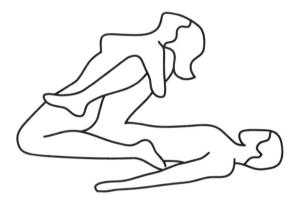

CALORIES

Him 134.4

Her 96

○ Below Average

○ Average

○ Above Average

○ Whoa!

COMMENTS

THE HONEYMOON IN MASSACHUSETTS

CALORIES

Giver 134

Receiver 75.6

EQUIPMENT

Chair

Chocolates

Roses

○ Below Average

○ Average

○ Above Average

○ Whoa!

COMMENTS

AUGUST 23)
THE RUNAWAY BRIDE

CALORIES

Him 75.6

Her 54

○ Below Average

○ Average

○ Above Average

○ Whoa!

COMMENTS

AUGUST 24)
THE SOMETHING TO FALL
BACK ON

CALORIES
Him 67.2
Her 54

EQUIPMENT
Chair

○ Below Average
○ Average
○ Above Average
○ Whoa!

COMMENTS

AUGUST 25)
THE MILKMAN COMETH

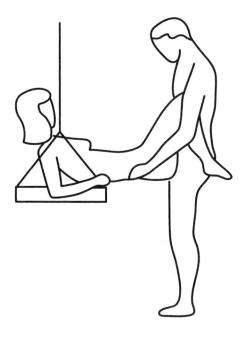

CALORIES

Him 75.6

Her 66

EQUIPMENT

Porch Swing

○ Below Average

○ Average

○ Above Average

○ Whoa!

COMMENTS

AUGUST 26)
THE SIDE SPLITTER

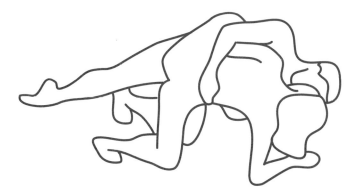

CALORIES

Him 117.6

Her 54

○ Below Average

○ Average

○ Above Average

○ Whoa!

COMMENTS

AUGUST 27)
INNER PIECE

CALORIES
Him 19
Her 54

EQUIPMENT
Optional:
Indian Flute
Music

BENEFIT
Enlightenment

○ Below Average
○ Average
○ Above Average
○ Whoa!

COMMENTS

LEGS OVER EASY

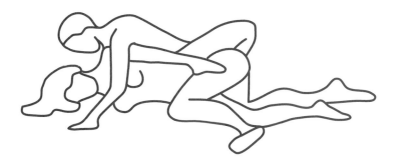

CALORIES

Him 75.6

Her   48

○ Below Average

○ Average

○ Above Average

○ Whoa!

COMMENTS

AUGUST 29)
WATCHING THE BOOB TUBE

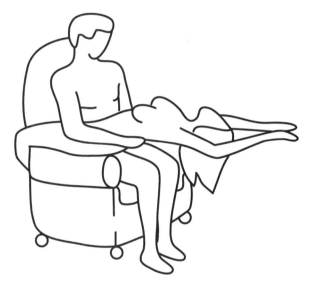

CALORIES
Him 54
Her 63

EQUIPMENT
Chair

○ Below Average
○ Average
○ Above Average
○ Whoa!

COMMENTS

THE GOOD SPANKING

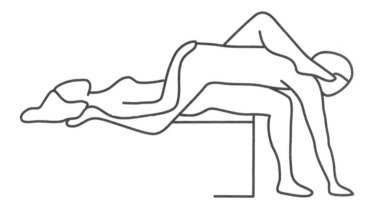

CALORIES
Him 67.2
Her 48

EQUIPMENT
Bed

○ Below Average
○ Average
○ Above Average
○ Whoa!

COMMENTS

AUGUST 31)
THE PICKUP ARTIST

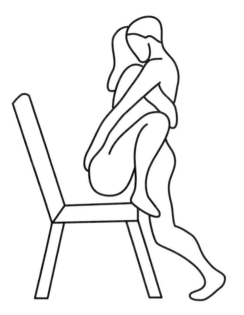

CALORIES **EQUIPMENT** **HAZARD**

Him 94   Chair   Obesity

Her 57

○ Below Average

○ Average

○ Above Average

○ Whoa!

COMMENTS

SEPTEMBER 01)
THE RUNNER'S KNEE

CALORIES

Him 75.6

Her 54

○ Below Average

○ Average

○ Above Average

○ Whoa!

COMMENTS

SEPTEMBER 02)
THE IMPROVIZED BED

CALORIES
Him 37
Her 61

EQUIPMENT
Two Chairs

○ Below Average
○ Average
○ Above Average
○ Whoa!

COMMENTS

SEPTEMBER 03)
THE BREAST EXAM

CALORIES
Him 75.6
Her 66

EQUIPMENT
Pull-up Bar

○ Below Average
○ Average
○ Above Average
○ Whoa!

COMMENTS

SEPTEMBER 04)
SHIFTING INTO DRIVE

CALORIES

Him 45

Her 75

○ Below Average

○ Average

○ Above Average

○ Whoa!

COMMENTS

SEPTEMBER 05)
THE HEAD OVER HEELS

CALORIES

Him 78

Her 45

○ Below Average

○ Average

○ Above Average

○ Whoa!

COMMENTS

SEPTEMBER 06)
THE LIFT FROM YOUR KNEES

CALORIES

Him 98

Her 62

○ Below Average

○ Average

○ Above Average

○ Whoa!

COMMENTS

SEPTEMBER 07)
THE THIGH MASTER

CALORIES

Him 75.6

Her 58

EQUIPMENT

Rocking Chair

○ Below Average

○ Average

○ Above Average

○ Whoa!

COMMENTS

SEPTEMBER 08)
THE DOG ON THE PORCH

CALORIES

Him 75.6

Her 66

EQUIPMENT

Porch Swing

○ Below Average

○ Average

○ Above Average

○ Whoa!

COMMENTS

SEPTEMBER 09)
THE "DROP ME AND I'LL SUE"

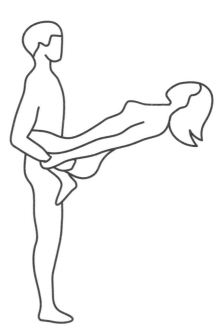

CALORIES
Him 100.8
Her 132

EQUIPMENT
Lawyer

○ Below Average
○ Average
○ Above Average
○ Whoa!

COMMENTS

SEPTEMBER 10)
YOU'RE HIRED

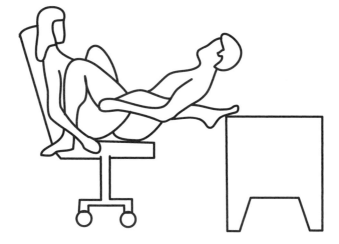

CALORIES
Him 67.2
Her 48

EQUIPMENT
Office
Chair
Desk

BENEFIT
Glowing Job
Reference

○ Below Average
○ Average
○ Above Average
○ Whoa!

COMMENTS

THE HAPPY EXISTENTIALISTS

CALORIES

Him 19

Her 23.6

○ Below Average
○ Average
○ Above Average
○ Whoa!

COMMENTS

_____
_____
_____
_____
_____

SEPTEMBER 12)
THE HEDGE TRIMMER

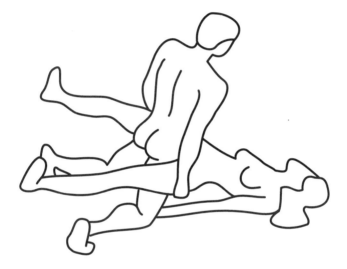

CALORIES

Him 75.6

Her 13.6

○ Below Average
○ Average
○ Above Average
○ Whoa!

COMMENTS

SEPTEMBER 13)
THE "NOT SURE WE'RE DOING THIS RIGHT"

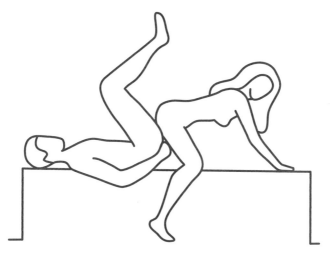

CALORIES	EQUIPMENT	
Him 75.6	Bench	○ Below Average
Her 54		○ Average
		○ Above Average
		○ Whoa!

COMMENTS

SEPTEMBER 14)
THE DUMB AND DUMBER

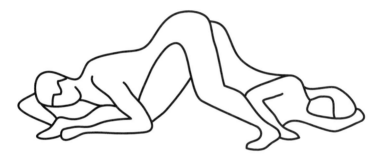

CALORIES

Him 75.6

Her 54

○ Below Average
○ Average
○ Above Average
○ Whoa!

COMMENTS

SEPTEMBER 15)
WHEN HARRY MET SALLY AND FRANK

CALORIES

Him (Standing) 88

Her 71

Him 73

○ Below Average

○ Average

○ Above Average

○ Whoa!

COMMENTS

SEPTEMBER 16)
ON YOUR MARK

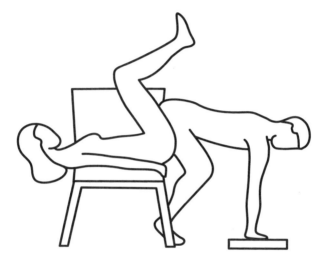

CALORIES

Him 134.4

Her 96

EQUIPMENT

Chair

Stool

Optional: Start Gun

○ Below Average

○ Average

○ Above Average

○ Whoa!

COMMENTS

THE WE SHOULD REALLY TALK

CALORIES

Him 75.6

Her 48

EQUIPMENT

Bed

○ Below Average

○ Average

○ Above Average

○ Whoa!

COMMENTS

SEPTEMBER 18)
LICK MY NECK...

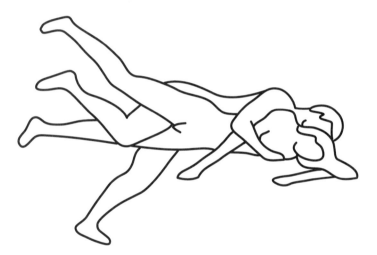

CALORIES

Him 75

Her 66

○ Below Average
○ Average
○ Above Average
○ Whoa!

COMMENTS

THE "I GUESS THEY'RE RIGHT ABOUT FOOT SIZE AND..."

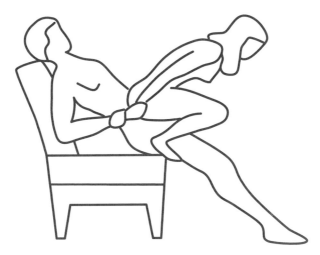

CALORIES

Him 75.6

Her 54

EQUIPMENT

Nice Shoes

Chair

○ Below Average

○ Average

○ Above Average

○ Whoa!

COMMENTS

SEPTEMBER 20)
THE GRIEF COUNSELOR

CALORIES

Him 75.6

Her 54

EQUIPMENT

Wall

Tissues

○ Below Average

○ Average

○ Above Average

○ Whoa!

COMMENTS

CALORIES	EQUIPMENT	
Him 75.6	Pillow	○ Below Average
Her 96		○ Average
		○ Above Average
		○ Whoa!

COMMENTS

SEPTEMBER 22)
THE HANG ON LUCY,
LUCY HANG ON

CALORIES

Him 75.6

Her 96

EQUIPMENT

Pull-up Bar

○ Below Average

○ Average

○ Above Average

○ Whoa!

COMMENTS

SEPTEMBER 23)
THE "EX-CELLENT!"

CALORIES
Him 19
Her 84

EQUIPMENT
Chair

○ Below Average
○ Average
○ Above Average
○ Whoa!

COMMENTS

SEPTEMBER 24)
LATE NIGHT AT HOGWARTS

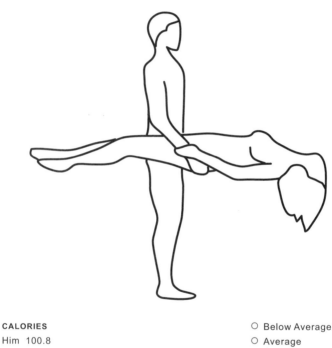

CALORIES

Him 100.8

Her 96

○ Below Average

○ Average

○ Above Average

○ Whoa!

COMMENTS

CALORIES

Him 67.2

Her 54

EQUIPMENT

Rocking Chair

Stool

Video

HAZARD

Depressing Movies

○ Below Average

○ Average

○ Above Average

○ Whoa!

COMMENTS

SEPTEMBER 26)
THE "JUST TRUST ME ON THIS ONE"

CALORIES
Him 84
Her 60

EQUIPMENT
Rocking Chair

BENEFIT
Sore Elbows
Loss of Trust

○ Below Average
○ Average
○ Above Average
○ Whoa!

COMMENTS

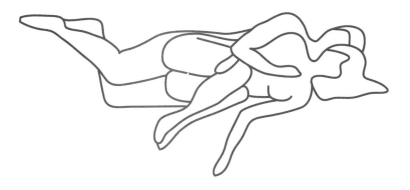

CALORIES

Him 75.6

Her   95

○ Below Average

○ Average

○ Above Average

○ Whoa!

COMMENTS

SEPTEMBER 28)
THE CHARLIE HORSE

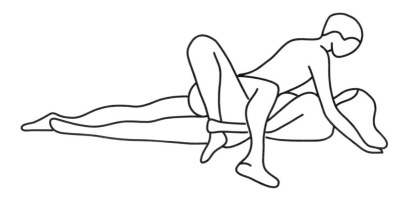

CALORIES

Him 67.2

Her 48

○ Below Average

○ Average

○ Above Average

○ Whoa!

COMMENTS

THE UNDERSTUDY

CALORIES

Him 19

Her 54

○ Below Average

○ Average

○ Above Average

○ Whoa!

COMMENTS

SEPTEMBER 30)
THE CO-ED JV
WRESTLING TEAM

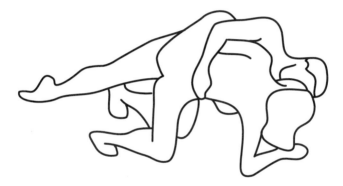

CALORIES

Him 117.6

Her 54

○ Below Average

○ Average

○ Above Average

○ Whoa!

COMMENTS

THE HOTDOG AND A PRETZEL

CALORIES

Him 67

Her 49

○ Below Average

○ Average

○ Above Average

○ Whoa!

COMMENTS

OCTOBER 02)
THE "GIVE ME AN A"

CALORIES

Him 100.8

Her 96

○ Below Average

○ Average

○ Above Average

○ Whoa!

COMMENTS

OCTOBER 03)
THE "I'M EVERY WOMAN"

CALORIES

Him 67.2

Her 96

HAZARD

Narcissism

○ Below Average

○ Average

○ Above Average

○ Whoa!

COMMENTS

OCTOBER 04)
3-2-1 BLASTOFF

CALORIES

Him 19

Her 54

○ Below Average

○ Average

○ Above Average

○ Whoa!

COMMENTS

_____
_____
_____
_____
_____

OCTOBER 05)
THE "THAT'S AS FAR AS IT GOES"

CALORIES

Him 75.6

Her 54

○ Below Average

○ Average

○ Above Average

○ Whoa!

COMMENTS

OCTOBER 06)
THE SYNCHRONIZED SWIM

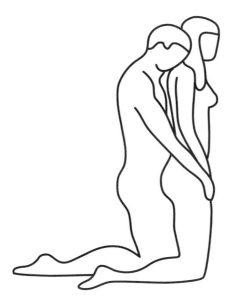

CALORIES

Him 75.6

Her 54

○ Below Average

○ Average

○ Above Average

○ Whoa!

COMMENTS

OCTOBER 07)
THE SO CLOSE AND YET SO FAR

CALORIES

Him 75.6

Her 96

○ Below Average

○ Average

○ Above Average

○ Whoa!

COMMENTS

_____

_____

_____

_____

_____

_____

OCTOBER 08)
THE PAUSE THAT REFRESHES

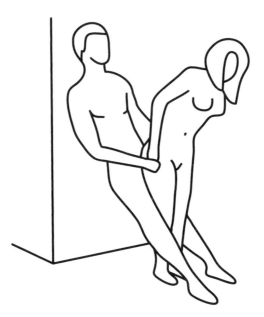

CALORIES
Him 50.4
Her 54

EQUIPMENT
Wall

○ Below Average
○ Average
○ Above Average
○ Whoa!

COMMENTS

THE SEABISCUIT

CALORIES
Him 168
Her   48

○ Below Average
○ Average
○ Above Average
○ Whoa!

COMMENTS
_____
_____
_____
_____
_____
_____

OCTOBER 10)
MAKING HER STAND

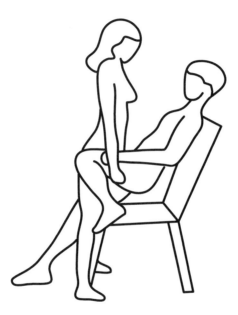

CALORIES
Him 55
Her 60

EQUIPMENT
Chair

○ Below Average
○ Average
○ Above Average
○ Whoa!

COMMENTS

THE NO PAIN NO GAIN

CALORIES	EQUIPMENT	
Him 67.2	Advil	○ Below Average
Her 54	Ice Pack	○ Average
		○ Above Average
		○ Whoa!

COMMENTS

OCTOBER 12)
WAGGING THE DOG

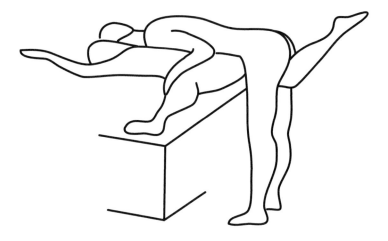

CALORIES
Him 75.6
Her 66

EQUIPMENT
Bed

BENEFIT
Increased Flexibility

○ Below Average
○ Average
○ Above Average
○ Whoa!

COMMENTS

THE AFTERNOON DELIGHT

CALORIES	EQUIPMENT	
Him 75.6	Pillow	○ Below Average
Her 96		○ Average
		○ Above Average
		○ Whoa!

COMMENTS

THE TONGUE IN CHEEK

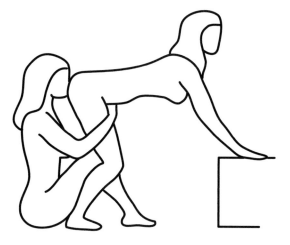

CALORIES

Giver   13.6

Receiver 48

EQUIPMENT

Bed

○ Below Average

○ Average

○ Above Average

○ Whoa!

COMMENTS

OCTOBER 15)
THE SUNDAY PAPER

CALORIES
Him 67.2
Her 48

EQUIPMENT
Newspaper

○ Below Average
○ Average
○ Above Average
○ Whoa!

COMMENTS

OCTOBER 16)
THE SLIP SLIDIN' AWAY

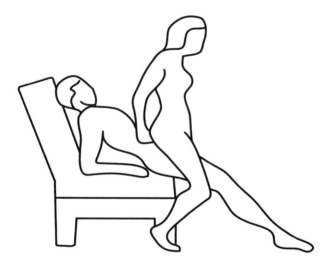

CALORIES

Him 75.6

Her 54

EQUIPMENT

Chair

HAZARD

Stop Immediately if
You Hear a Snapping
Sound

○ Below Average

○ Average

○ Above Average

○ Whoa!

COMMENTS

OCTOBER 17)
THE TRUST FALL

CALORIES	EQUIPMENT	BENEFIT	
Him 117.6	Rocking Chair	New Sense of Trust	○ Below Average
Her 84	Optional:	in Relationship	○ Average
	Insurance		○ Above Average
			○ Whoa!

COMMENTS

OCTOBER 18)
THE VERY CURIOUS GEORGE

CALORIES

Him 134.4

Her 54

EQUIPMENT

Doorframe

Pull-up Bar

Stool

○ Below Average

○ Average

○ Above Average

○ Whoa!

COMMENTS

OCTOBER 19)
THE FOOT WARMER

CALORIES

Him 117.6

Her   96

○ Below Average

○ Average

○ Above Average

○ Whoa!

COMMENTS

OCTOBER 20)
THE DEN OF INIQUITY

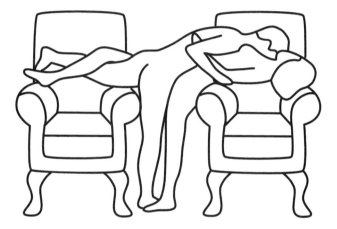

CALORIES   **EQUIPMENT**

Him 92.4   Two Chairs

Her 84

○ Below Average

○ Average

○ Above Average

○ Whoa!

COMMENTS

BILL AND TED'S EXCELLENT ADVENTURE

CALORIES

Giver   75.6

Receiver 66

EQUIPMENT

Two Chairs

○ Below Average
○ Average
○ Above Average
○ Whoa!

COMMENTS

OCTOBER 22)
THE I'LL TAKE THE FRONT, YOU TAKE THE BACK

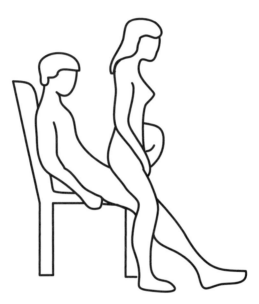

CALORIES

Him 19

Her 84

EQUIPMENT

Chair

○ Below Average

○ Average

○ Above Average

○ Whoa!

COMMENTS

OCTOBER 23)
THE FIDDLER UNDER THE ROOF

CALORIES

Him 54

Her   19

○ Below Average

○ Average

○ Above Average

○ Whoa!

COMMENTS

OCTOBER 24)
THE DIVING INSTRUCTOR

CALORIES

Him 76.6

Her 54

EQUIPMENT

Stool

○ Below Average

○ Average

○ Above Average

○ Whoa!

COMMENTS

OCTOBER 25)
DEBBIE DOES DEBBIE

CALORIES

Giver   13.6

Receiver 54

○ Below Average

○ Average

○ Above Average

○ Whoa!

COMMENTS

OCTOBER 26)
THE PINOCCHIO

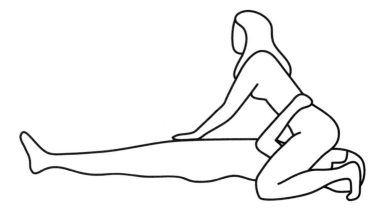

CALORIES

Him 19

Her 48

○ Below Average

○ Average

○ Above Average

○ Whoa!

COMMENTS

_____

_____

_____

_____

_____

THE SCHOOL OF ROCK

CALORIES	EQUIPMENT	
Him 67.2	Rocking Chair	○ Below Average
Her 54		○ Average
		○ Above Average
		○ Whoa!

COMMENTS

OCTOBER 28)
THE BUTLER DID IT

CALORIES

Him 100.8

Her 96

○ Below Average
○ Average
○ Above Average
○ Whoa!

COMMENTS

OCTOBER 29)
REACH OUT AND TOUCH SOMEONE

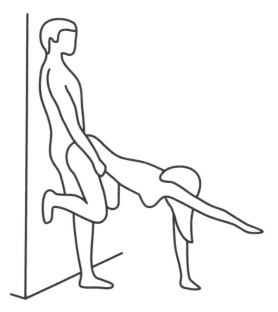

CALORIES
Him 50.4
Her 96

EQUIPMENT
Wall

○ Below Average
○ Average
○ Above Average
○ Whoa!

COMMENTS

OCTOBER 30)
THE WAIT A MINUTE, MR. POSTMAN

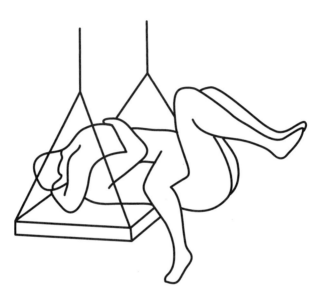

CALORIES
Him 75.6
Her 66

EQUIPMENT
Porch Swing
Mailbag

BENEFIT
No Mail Delays

○ Below Average
○ Average
○ Above Average
○ Whoa!

COMMENTS

OCTOBER 31)
CARVING THE HALLOWEEN PUMPKIN

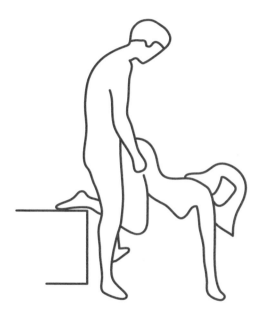

CALORIES	EQUIPMENT	BENEFIT	
Him 78	Bed	No Costume Necessary	○ Below Average
Her 62			○ Average
			○ Above Average
			○ Whoa!

COMMENTS

NOVEMBER 01)
THE CHUTES AND LADDERS

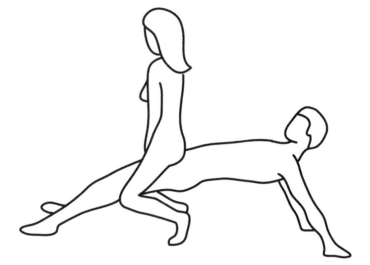

CALORIES

Him 168

Her 54

○ Below Average
○ Average
○ Above Average
○ Whoa!

COMMENTS

NOVEMBER 02)
TIT FOR TAT

CALORIES
Him 75.4
Her 56

EQUIPMENT
Stool

○ Below Average
○ Average
○ Above Average
○ Whoa!

COMMENTS

PATTING PATTY'S CAKES

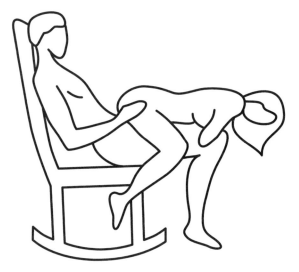

CALORIES

Him 19

Her 54

EQUIPMENT

Rocking Chair

O Below Average

O Average

O Above Average

O Whoa!

COMMENTS

NOVEMBER 04)
ROW ROW ROW YOUR BOAT

CALORIES

Him 117.6

Her 118

EQUIPMENT

Rocking Chair

○ Below Average

○ Average

○ Above Average

○ Whoa!

COMMENTS

NOVEMBER 05)
THE MARY LOU RETTON

CALORIES

Him 75.6

Her 92

EQUIPMENT

Bed

Optional: Leotard

○ Below Average

○ Average

○ Above Average

○ Whoa!

COMMENTS

CALORIES
Him 37
Her 61

EQUIPMENT
Two Chairs

HAZARD
Short Meetings

○ Below Average
○ Average
○ Above Average
○ Whoa!

COMMENTS

NOVEMBER 07)
HUT HUT HIKE

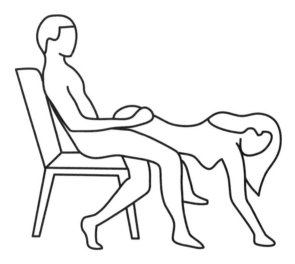

CALORIES
Him 19
Her 48

EQUIPMENT
Chair
Optional: Helmets,
Football Uniforms

HAZARD
Jock Strap

○ Below Average
○ Average
○ Above Average
○ Whoa!

COMMENTS

NOVEMBER 08)
THE "THIS JUST ISN'T WORKING OUT"

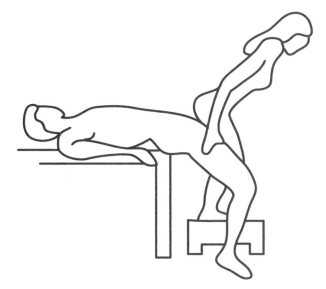

CALORIES	EQUIPMENT	HAZARD	
Him 19	Table	Take All Your Things Before Leaving	○ Below Average
Her 120	Stool		○ Average
			○ Above Average
			○ Whoa!

COMMENTS

_____
_____
_____
_____
_____

TIPPING THE MOVER

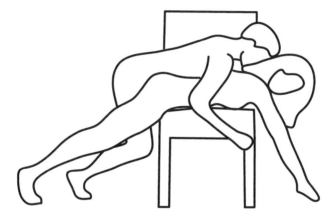

CALORIES
Him 75.6
Her 54

EQUIPMENT
Chair

○ Below Average
○ Average
○ Above Average
○ Whoa!

COMMENTS

NOVEMBER 10)
WE LOVE TO FLY AND IT SHOWS

CALORIES
Him 100.8
Her   132

○ Below Average
○ Average
○ Above Average
○ Whoa!

COMMENTS

NOVEMBER 11)
THE "SO, WHAT'S FOR DINNER?"

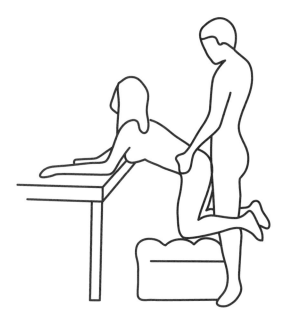

CALORIES
Him 67.2
Her 48

EQUIPMENT
Table
Ottoman

○ Below Average
○ Average
○ Above Average
○ Whoa!

COMMENTS

NOVEMBER 12)
OFFICE HOURS

CALORIES	EQUIPMENT	
Him 13.6	Office, Chair	O Below Average
Her 67.2	Optional:	O Average
	Tweed Jacket	O Above Average
		O Whoa!

COMMENTS

NOVEMBER 13)
THE FLIP IT 'N' REVERSE IT

CALORIES　　**HAZARD**

Him 19　　Smelly Feet

Her 13.6

○ Below Average

○ Average

○ Above Average

○ Whoa!

COMMENTS

_____

_____

_____

_____

_____

_____

NOVEMBER 14)
THE PARENT/TEACHER CONFERENCE

CALORIES
Him 58
Her 65

EQUIPMENT
Chair
Optional: Ruler

BENEFIT
Good Grades

○ Below Average
○ Average
○ Above Average
○ Whoa!

COMMENTS

NOVEMBER 15)
THE BREAKFAST OF CHAMPIONS

CALORIES

Giver 19

Receiver 13.6

EQUIPMENT

Wall

○ Below Average
○ Average
○ Above Average
○ Whoa!

COMMENTS

NOVEMBER 16)
THE HAND WARMER

CALORIES	EQUIPMENT	
Him 19	Rocking Chair	O Below Average
Her 60		O Average
		O Above Average
		O Whoa!

COMMENTS

NOVEMBER 17)
THE CAN I PLEASE TURN
AROUND NOW?

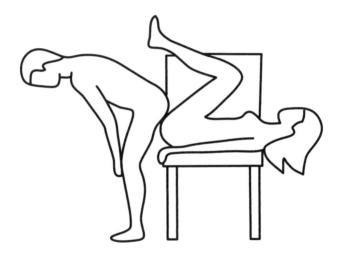

CALORIES

Him 75.6

Her 54

EQUIPMENT

Chair

○ Below Average

○ Average

○ Above Average

○ Whoa!

COMMENTS

NOVEMBER 18)
THE FINGER LICKIN' GOOD

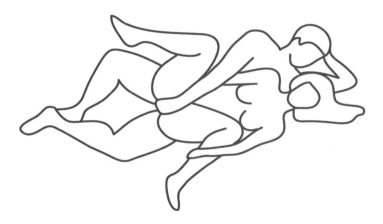

CALORIES

Him 35

Her 22

O Below Average

O Average

O Above Average

O Whoa!

COMMENTS

NOVEMBER 19)
THE SUN SALUTATION

CALORIES
Him 62
Her 49

EQUIPMENT
Pillow

O Below Average
O Average
O Above Average
O Whoa!

COMMENTS

NOVEMBER 20)
THE "WHEEEE"

CALORIES	EQUIPMENT	
Him 117.6	Rocking Chair	O Below Average
Her 120		O Average
		O Above Average
		O Whoa!

COMMENTS

NOVEMBER 21)
THE NICE MAN AT THE
BUS STOP

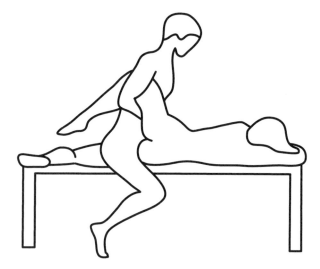

CALORIES
Him 75.6
Her 48

EQUIPMENT
Bench

○ Below Average
○ Average
○ Above Average
○ Whoa!

COMMENTS

CALORIES

Him 100.8

Her 96

EQUIPMENT

Pocket Watch with Chain

○ Below Average

○ Average

○ Above Average

○ Whoa!

COMMENTS

NOVEMBER 23)
THE SCRUNCHEE

CALORIES

Him 75.6

Her 54

○ Below Average
○ Average
○ Above Average
○ Whoa!

COMMENTS

NOVEMBER 24)
THE KINDNESS OF STRANGERS

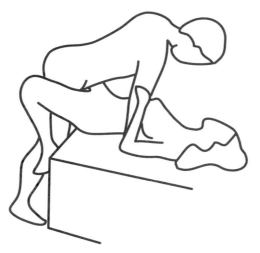

CALORIES

Him 75.6

Her 54

EQUIPMENT

Bed

○ Below Average

○ Average

○ Above Average

○ Whoa!

COMMENTS

NOVEMBER 25)
THE BLIND GYNECOLOGIST

CALORIES

Him 67.2

Her 96

○ Below Average
○ Average
○ Above Average
○ Whoa!

COMMENTS

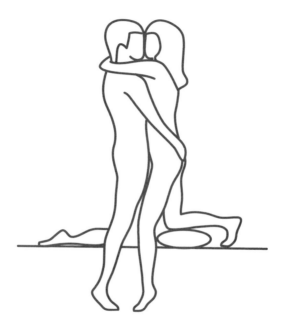

CALORIES
Him 19.19
Her 13.6

EQUIPMENT
Bench
Pillow

○ Below Average
○ Average
○ Above Average
○ Whoa!

COMMENTS

NOVEMBER 27)
THE MOMA INSTALLATION

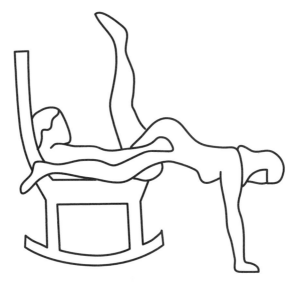

CALORIES
Him 50
Her 78

EQUIPMENT
Rocking Chair

○ Below Average
○ Average
○ Above Average
○ Whoa!

COMMENTS

THE COMPLEXITY OF DESIRE

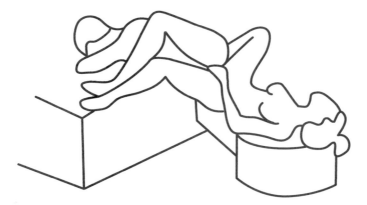

CALORIES	EQUIPMENT	
Him 75.6	Stool	○ Below Average
Her 48	Bed	○ Average
		○ Above Average
		○ Whoa!

COMMENTS

NOVEMBER 29)
THE RUBBER DUCKY

CALORIES
Him 72
Her 56

EQUIPMENT
Rocking Chair

○ Below Average
○ Average
○ Above Average
○ Whoa!

COMMENTS

AS HE LAY DYING

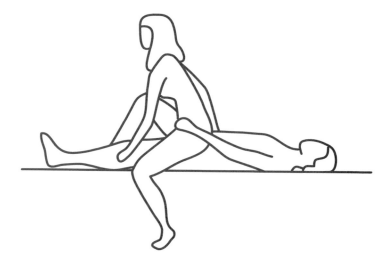

CALORIES

Him 19

Her   48

○ Below Average
○ Average
○ Above Average
○ Whoa!

COMMENTS

DECEMBER 01)
THE HEADACHE CURE

CALORIES

Him 75.6

Her 58

EQUIPMENT

Rocking Chair

Stool

BENEFIT

Saves Money on
Advil

○ Below Average

○ Average

○ Above Average

○ Whoa!

COMMENTS

DECEMBER 02)
THE LEAKING BLOW-UP DOLL

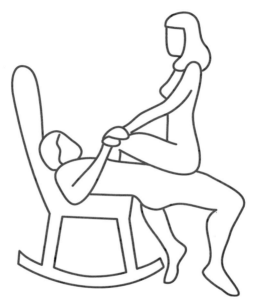

CALORIES
Him 19
Her 66

EQUIPMENT
Rocking Chair

O Below Average
O Average
O Above Average
O Whoa!

COMMENTS

DECEMBER 03)
SO THEY ALL ROLLED OVER...

CALORIES

Him 67.2

Her 48

○ Below Average
○ Average
○ Above Average
○ Whoa!

COMMENTS

DECEMBER 04)
THE NURSING AIDE

CALORIES
Him 19
Her 54

EQUIPMENT
Rocking Chair

HAZARD
Sudden Rise in
Blood Pressure

○ Below Average
○ Average
○ Above Average
○ Whoa!

COMMENTS

DECEMBER 05)
THE SNOWBALL EFFECT

CALORIES

Him 67.2

Her 48

○ Below Average
○ Average
○ Above Average
○ Whoa!

COMMENTS

DECEMBER 06)
DRIVING MS. DAISY

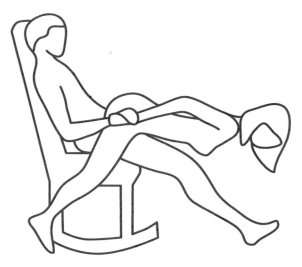

CALORIES	EQUIPMENT	
Him 19	Rocking Chair	O Below Average
Her 48		O Average
		O Above Average
		O Whoa!

COMMENTS

DECEMBER 07)
THE CATCH ME I'M FALLING

CALORIES   **EQUIPMENT**

Him 100.8   Bed

Her 96

○ Below Average

○ Average

○ Above Average

○ Whoa!

COMMENTS

DECEMBER 08)
THE ANXIOUS HONEYMOONER

CALORIES
Him 55
Her 40

EQUIPMENT
Doorframe

O Below Average
O Average
O Above Average
O Whoa!

COMMENTS

DECEMBER 09)
THE OTTO-MOM

CALORIES

Him 84

Her 54

EQUIPMENT

Ottoman

O Below Average

O Average

O Above Average

O Whoa!

COMMENTS

DECEMBER 10)
THE CRACK ADDICT

CALORIES
Him 19
Her   66

○ Below Average
○ Average
○ Above Average
○ Whoa!

COMMENTS

DECEMBER 11)
THE SPOON SWOON

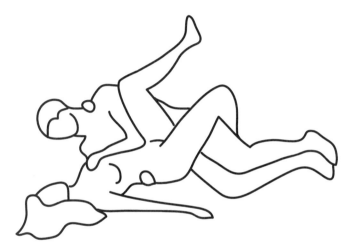

CALORIES

Him 75.6

Her 54

O Below Average

O Average

O Above Average

O Whoa!

COMMENTS

DECEMBER 12)
THE VERY FREUDIAN ANALYST

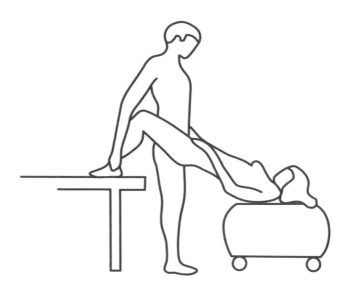

CALORIES	EQUIPMENT	BENEFIT	
Him 75.6	Table	Analyst Finally Responds	O Below Average
Her 96	Ottoman		O Average
			O Above Average
			O Whoa!

COMMENTS

DECEMBER 13)
THE PILE DRIVE-HER

CALORIES

Him 75.6

Her 54

HAZARD

Paralysis

O Below Average

O Average

O Above Average

O Whoa!

COMMENTS

DECEMBER 14)
THE SEX NAZI

CALORIES	EQUIPMENT
Him 67.2	Stool
Her 96	Wall

○ Below Average
○ Average
○ Above Average
○ Whoa!

COMMENTS

DECEMBER 15)
ADVANCED TIC-TAC-TOE

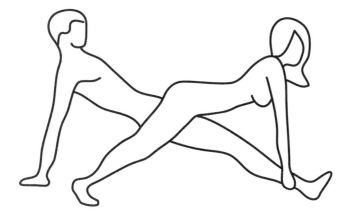

CALORIES

Him 134.4

Her 96

○ Below Average

○ Average

○ Above Average

○ Whoa!

COMMENTS

DECEMBER 16)
YOU BLINKED

CALORIES

Him 39

Her 28

○ Below Average
○ Average
○ Above Average
○ Whoa!

COMMENTS

DECEMBER 17)
THE TICKLE TORTURE

CALORIES

Him 75.6

Her 54

EQUIPMENT

Wall

O Below Average

O Average

O Above Average

O Whoa!

COMMENTS

DECEMBER 18)
FIRING THE HUMAN CANNONBALL

CALORIES	EQUIPMENT	
Him 100.8	Six-pack	○ Below Average
Her 132	Helmet	○ Average
		○ Above Average
		○ Whoa!

COMMENTS

DECEMBER 19)
THE TEXAS HOLD-HIM

CALORIES

Him 100.8

Her 66

○ Below Average

○ Average

○ Above Average

○ Whoa!

COMMENTS

_____

_____

_____

_____

_____

_____

DECEMBER 20)
THE ASKING YOUR EX
TO LEAVE

CALORIES

Him 134.4

Her 72

O Below Average

O Average

O Above Average

O Whoa!

COMMENTS

DECEMBER 21)
THE VERY PHYSICAL
THERAPIST

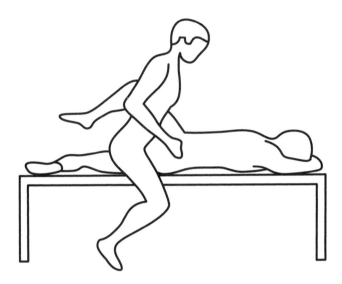

CALORIES
Him 75.6
Her   19

EQUIPMENT
Lotion
Massage Table

BENEFIT
Loose Muscles

○ Below Average
○ Average
○ Above Average
○ Whoa!

COMMENTS

DECEMBER 22)
THE HAZING RITUAL

CALORIES

Giver   134

Receiver   75.6

○ Below Average

○ Average

○ Above Average

○ Whoa!

COMMENTS

DECEMBER 23)
THE PRE-GAME WARMUP

CALORIES
Him 67.2
Her 66

EQUIPMENT
Bench
Optional:
Pull-Off Basketball Jumpsuit

BENEFIT
Loose Hamstrings

○ Below Average
○ Average
○ Above Average
○ Whoa!

COMMENTS

DECEMBER 24)
THE NOSY NEIGHBOR

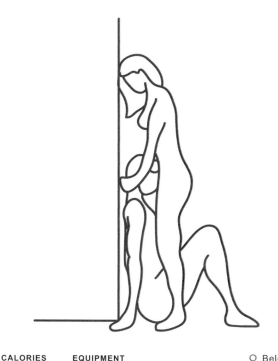

CALORIES
Him 19
Her 48

EQUIPMENT
Wall

O Below Average
O Average
O Above Average
O Whoa!

COMMENTS

DECEMBER 25)
THE MERRY X-MAS

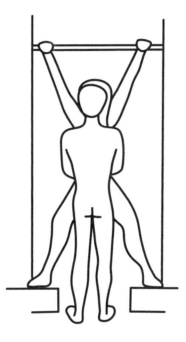

CALORIES
Him 75.6
Her 48

EQUIPMENT
Pull-up Bar
Doorframe
Two Stools

BENEFIT
No Christmas
Shopping

○ Below Average
○ Average
○ Above Average
○ Whoa!

COMMENTS

DECEMBER 26)
THE TRIPOD

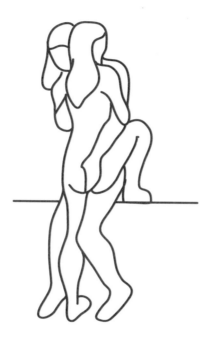

CALORIES
Her (One-Legged) 72
Her (Two-Legged) 55

EQUIPMENT
Bed

○ Below Average
○ Average
○ Above Average
○ Whoa!

COMMENTS

DECEMBER 27)
THE EVERYTHING'S GONNA BE ALRIGHT

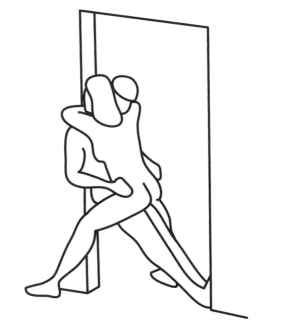

CALORIES
Him 66
Her 75.6

EQUIPMENT
Doorframe

○ Below Average
○ Average
○ Above Average
○ Whoa!

COMMENTS

THE BEAST WITH TWO BACKS

CALORIES

Him 84

Her   61

○ Below Average

○ Average

○ Above Average

○ Whoa!

COMMENTS

DECEMBER 29)
THE DOG ON THE CHAIR

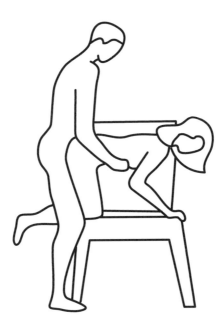

CALORIES

Him 72

Her 56

EQUIPMENT

Chair

O Below Average

O Average

O Above Average

O Whoa!

COMMENTS

DECEMBER 30)
THE RAW BAR

CALORIES
Him 19
Her 48

○ Below Average
○ Average
○ Above Average
○ Whoa!

COMMENTS

DECEMBER 31)
SHOULD AULD
ACQUAINTANCE BE FORGOT

CALORIES

Him 19

Her 39

○ Below Average

○ Average

○ Above Average

○ Whoa!

COMMENTS

COMMENTS